Jews

IN MINNESOTA

Hyman Berman and Linda Mack Schloff

Foreword by Bill Holm

 MINNESOTA HISTORICAL SOCIETY PRESS

Publication of this book was supported, in part, with funds provided by the June D. Holm-quist Publication Endowment Fund of the Minnesota Historical Society.

www.mnhs.org/mhspress

Manufactured in Canada

10 9 8 7 6 5 4 3 2 1

International Standard Book Number: 0-87351-418-1

♾ The paper used in this publication meets the minimum requirements of the American National Standard for Information Sciences Permanence for Printed Library Materials, ANSI Z39.48-1984.

Library of Congress Cataloging-in-Publication Data

Berman, Hyman, 1925–
    Jews in Minnesota / Hyman Berman and Linda Mack Schloff ; foreword by Bill Holm.
        p.   cm. — (The people of Minnesota)
    Includes bibliographical references and index.
    ISBN 0-87351-418-1 (pbk. : alk. paper)
        1. Jews—Minnesota—History. 2. Minnesota—Ethnic relations. I. Schloff, Linda Mack.
    II. Title. III. Series.

F615.J5 B47 2002
977.6004'924—dc21

                                                                              2002016505

This book was designed and set in type by Wendy Holdman, Stanton Publication Services, Saint Paul, Minnesota; and was printed by Friesens, Altona, Manitoba.

Contents

Foreword

by Bill Holm

Human beings have not been clever students at learning any lessons from their three or four thousand odd years of recorded history. We repeat our mistakes from generation to generation with tedious regularity. But we ought to have learned at least one simple truth: that there is no word, no idea that is not a double-edged sword. Take, for example, the adjective *ethnic.* In one direction, it cuts upward, to show us the faces, the lives, the histories of our neighbors and ourselves. It shows us that we are not alone on this planet—that we are all rooted with deep tendrils growing down to our ancestors and the stories of how they came to be not *there,* but *here.* These tendrils are visible in our noses and cheekbones, our middle-aged diseases and discomforts, our food, our religious habits, our celebrations, our manner of grieving, our very names. The fact that here in Minnesota, at any rate, we mostly live together in civil harmony—showing sometimes affectionate curiosity, sometimes puzzled irritation but seldom murderous violence—speaks well for our progress as a community of neighbors, even as members of a civilized human tribe.

But early in this new century in America we have seen the dark blade of the ethnic sword made visible, and it has cut us to the quick. From at least one angle, our national wounds from terrorist attacks are an example of ethnicity gone mad, tribal loyalty whipped to fanatical hysteria, until it turns human beings into monstrous machines of mass murder. Few tribes own a guiltless history in this regard.

The 20th century did not see much progress toward solving the problem of ethnicity. Think of Turk and Armenian, German and Jew, Hutu and Tutsi, Protestant and Catholic, Albanian and Serb, French and Algerian—think of our own lynchings. We all hoped for better from the 21st century but may not get any reprieve at all from the tidal waves of violence and hatred.

As global capitalism breaks down the borders between nation-states, fanatical ethnicity rises to life like a hydra. Cheerful advertisements assure us that we are all a family—wearing the same pants, drinking the same pop, singing and going on line together as we spend. When we invoke *family,* we don't seen to remember well the ancient Greek family tragedies. We need to make not a family but a civil community of neighbors, who may neither spend nor look alike but share a desire for truthful history—an alert curiosity about the stories and the lives of our neighbors and a respect both for difference—and for privacy. We must get the metaphors right; we are neither brothers nor sisters here in Minnesota, nor even cousins. We are neighbors, all us *ethnics,* and that fact imposes on us a stricter obligation than blood and, to the degree to which we live up to it, makes us civilized.

As both Minnesotans and Americans, none of us can escape the fact that we *ethnics,* in historic terms, have hardly settled here for the length of a sneeze. Most of us have barely had time to lose the language of our ancestors or to produce protein-stuffed children half a foot taller than ourselves. What does a mere century or a little better amount to in history? Even the oldest settlers—the almost ur-inhabitants, the Dakota and Ojibwa—emigrated here from elsewhere on the continent. The Jeffers Petroglyphs in southwest Minnesota are probably the oldest evidence we have of any human habitation. They are still and will most likely remain only shadowy tellers of any historic truth about us. Who made this language? History is silent. The only clear facts scholars agree on about these mysterious pictures carved in hard red Sioux quartzite is that they were the work of neither of the current native tribes and can be scientifically dated only between the melting of the last glacier and the arrival of the first European settlers in the territory. They seem very old to the eye. It is good for us, I think, that our history begins not with certainty, but with mystery, cause for wonder rather than warfare.

In 1978, before the first edition of this ethnic survey appeared, a researcher came to Minneota to interview local people for information about the Icelanders. Tiny though their numbers, the Icelanders were a real ethnic group with their own language, history, and habits of mind. They settled in the late 19th century in three small clumps around Minneota. At that time, I could still introduce this researcher to a few old ladies born in Iceland and to a dozen children of immigrants who grew up with English as a second language, thus with thick accents. The old still prayed the Lord's Prayer in Icelandic, to them the language of Jesus himself, and a handful of people could still read the ancient poems and sagas in the leather-covered editions brought as treasures from the old country. But two decades have wiped out that primary source. The first generation is gone, only a few alert and alive in the second, and the third speaks only English—real Americans in hardly a century. What driblets of Icelandic blood remain are mixed with a little of this, a little of that. The old thorny names, so difficult to pronounce, have been respelled, then corrected for sound.

Is this the end of ethnicity? The complete meltdown into history evaporated into global marketing anonymity? I say no. On a late October day, a letter arrives from a housewife in Nevis, Minnesota. She's never met me, but she's been to Iceland now and met unknown cousins she found on an Internet genealogy search. The didactic voice in my books reminds her of her father's voice: "He could've said that. Are we *all* literary?" We've never met, she confesses, but she gives me enough of her family tree to convince me that we might be cousins fifteen generations back. She is descended, she says with pride, from the Icelandic law speaker in 1063, Gunnar the Wise. She knows now that she is not alone in history. She has shadowing names, even dates, in her very cells. She says—with more smug pride—that her vinarterta (an Icelandic immigrant prune cake that is often the last surviving ghost of the old country) is better than any she ate in Iceland. She invites me to sample a piece if I ever get to Nevis. Who says there is no profit and joy in ethnicity? That killjoy has obviously never tasted vinarterta!

I think what is happening in this letter, both psychologically and culturally, happens simultaneously in the lives of hundreds of thousands of Minnesotans and countless millions of Americans. Only the details differ, pilaf, jiaozi, fry bread, collards, latkes, or menudo rather than vinarterta, but the process and the object remain the same. We came to this cold flat place so far from the sea in wave after wave of immigration—filling up the steadily fewer empty places in this vast midsection of a continent—but for all of us, whatever the reason for our arrival: poverty, political upheaval, ambition—we check most of our history, and thus our inner life, at the door of the new world. For a while, old habits and even the language carry on, but by the third generation, history is lost. Yet America's history, much less Minnesota's, is so tiny, so new, so uncertain, so much composed of broken connections—and now of vapid media marketing—that we feel a loneliness for a history that stretches back further into the life of the planet. We want more cousins so that, in the best sense, we can be better neighbors. We can acquire interior weight that will keep us rooted in our new homes. That is why we need to read these essays on the ethnic history of Minnesota. We need to meet those neighbors and listen to new stories.

We need also the concrete underpinning of facts that they provide to give real body to our tribal myths if those myths are not to drift off into nostalgic vapor. Svenskarnas Dag and Santa Lucia Day will not tell us much about the old Sweden that disgorged so many of its poor to Minnesota. At the height of the Vietnam War, an old schoolmate of mine steeled his courage to confess to his stern Swedish father that he was thinking both of conscientious objection and, if that didn't work, escape to Canada. He expected patriotic disdain, even contempt. Instead the upright old man wept and cried, "So soon again!" He had left Sweden early in the century to avoid the compulsory military draft but told that history to none of his children. The history of our arrival here does not lose its nobility by being filled with draft-dodging, tubercular lungs, head lice, poverty, failure. It gains humanity. We are all members of a very big club—and not an exclusive one.

I grew up in western Minnesota surrounded by accents: Icelandic, Norwegian, Swedish, Belgian, Dutch, German, Polish, French Canadian, Irish, even a Yankee or two, a French Jewish doctor, and a Japanese chicken sexer in Dr. Kerr's chicken hatchery. As a boy, I thought that a fair-sized family of nations. Some of those tribes have declined almost to extinction, and new immigrants have come to replace them: Mexican, Somali, Hmong, and Balkan. Relations are sometimes awkward as the old ethnicities bump their aging dispositions against the new, forgetting that their own grandparents spoke English strangely, dressed in odd clothes, and ate foods that astonished and sometimes repulsed their neighbors. History does not cease moving at the exact moment we begin to occupy it comfortably.

I've taught many Laotian students in my freshman English classes at Southwest State University in Marshall. I always assign papers on family history. For many children of the fourth generation, the real stories have evaporated, but for the Hmong, they are very much alive—escape followed by gunfire, swimming the Mekong, a childhood in Thai refugee camps. One student brought a piece of his mother's intricate embroidery to class and translated its symbolic storytelling language for his class-mates. Those native-born children of farmers will now be haunted for life by the dark water of the Mekong. Ethnic history is alive and surprisingly well in Minnesota.

Meanwhile the passion for connection—thus a craving for a deeper history—has blossomed grandly in my generation and the new one in front of it. A Canadian professional genealogist at work at an immigrant genealogical center at Hofsos in north Iceland assures me, as fact, that genealogy has surpassed, in raw numbers, both stamp and coin collect-ing as a hobby. What will it next overtake? Baseball cards? Rock and roll 45 rpms? It's a sport with a future, and these essays on ethnic history are part of the evidence of its success.

I've even bought a little house in Hofsos, thirty miles south of the Arctic Circle where in the endless summer light I watch loads of immi-grant descendants from Canada and the United States arrive clutching old brown-tone photos, yellowed letters in languages they don't read, the misspelled name of Grandpa's farm. They feed their information into computers and comb through heavy books, hoping to find the history lost when their ancestors simplified their names at Ellis Island or in Que-bec. To be ethnic, somehow, is to be human. Neither can we escape it, nor should we want to. You cannot interest yourself in the lives of your neighbors if you don't take sufficient interest in your own.

Minnesotans often jokingly describe their ethnic backgrounds as "mongrel"—a little of this, a little of that, who knows what? But what a gift to be a mongrel! So many ethnicities and so little time in life to track them down! You will have to read many of these essays to find out who was up to what, when. We should also note that every one of us on this planet is a mongrel, thank God. The mongrel is the strongest and longest lived of dogs—and of humans, too. Only the dead are pure—and then, only in memory, never in fact. Mongrels do not kill each other to main-tain the pure ideology of the tribe. They just go on mating, acquiring a richer ethnic history with every passing generation. So I commend this series to you. Let me introduce you to your neighbors. May you find pleasure and wisdom in their company.

Jews

IN MINNESOTA

Children outside a kosher grocery store at 6th Avenue North and Lyndale, about 1909

"**B**UT WHEN WE STARTED up the river at noon on that bright May day I did not think that the time to go to 'the end of the world' had come so soon," Amelia Ullmann wrote of her trip from St. Louis to St. Paul in 1855. Nearly sixty years later Sam Char disembarked at St. Paul. He recalled that "the West Side did not make a good impression on me. There were no sidewalks and the street was not paved and there was mud all over." Despite depressing first impressions and an awareness of the hurdles they would face, they set to work re-creating Jewish homes and communities in a location so distant from established American Jewish population centers. The Ullmann family was among the settlers of Minnesota Territory soon after its creation in 1849. Despite their pioneer status, Jews have remained a small percentage of the total population. They were the merchants on Main Street in towns such as Virginia, Hibbing, Eveleth, Chisholm, Mankato, and Rochester. In all of these smaller cities, they were, in past generations, able to attract a critical mass, consisting at a minimum of a few families, to activate group life—to form religious congregations, burial societies, and fraternal and cultural institutions. But the majority of Jews, ones like Sam Char, chose to live in the commercial centers of the Twin Cities and Duluth. Here they were able to establish and maintain elaborate communal structures.[1]

The earliest Jewish settlers arrived in Minnesota from the eastern and southern United States, from central Europe (mostly the Germanic lands), and in small numbers from the western sections of eastern Europe. From the 1880s until the close of mass migration to the United States in the 1920s, Jews reached Minnesota largely from the Russian Empire's Pale of Settlement (Poland, Ukraine, White Russia or Belorus, and the Baltic provinces), from the Galician sections of the Austro-Hungarian Empire, and from

Romania. They emigrated as individuals and as families, driven from their homes by religious, cultural, political, economic, and social disabilities or attracted by opportunities in the New World.[2]

They arrived speaking German, Yiddish, Polish, Romanian, Russian, Hungarian, and a multiplicity of other languages. Most had left self-contained Yiddish-speaking urban village communities that were breaking down under the pressures of modernization and industrialization. Many, particularly those from eastern Europe, retained the cultural characteristics of Orthodox piety, including Old World styles of dress.[3]

The Jewish population of Minnesota reached an estimated peak of 43,700 in 1937. By 1995 approximately 42,000 Jews were counted in the state. Some 31,560 lived in Minneapolis and its suburbs, 11,100 in St. Paul and its suburbs, and about 1,000 in the Duluth area. Elsewhere only Virginia and Hibbing on the Mesabi Range and Austin and Rochester in southern Minnesota recorded more than 100 Jews. Thus, although they constituted only 0.9% of the total population of the state, they accounted for about 1.7% of the population of the Twin Cities metropolitan area.[4]

Controversy still abounds as to the definition of a Jew. Does religious affiliation determine identity? If so, what of those Jews who refused to participate in sacred institutions? How does one classify a person born of Jewish parents who converted to a Christian denomination or the children born of mixed marriages? Questions of this kind occur and recur to plague scholars who attempt to analyze the Jewish group experience.

Jews are a people with common historical and cultural traits as well as a shared core of religious identity. Some commentators identify Jews as a nation and others have erroneously called them a race. We have chosen to regard them as an ethnic group. Given the diversity of national origins, the heterogeneity of religious affiliations, the Babel of languages, and the complexities of diverse historical experiences, the only safe definition must be an eclectic one that depends upon self-perception. A person or group of people who identify themselves as Jews, participate in institutions or activities—religious, cultural, philanthropic, political, or social—that seek to perpetuate Jewish group identity will here be regarded as Jews.[5]

The Pioneer Era

Although at least one Jew was numbered among fur traders in the 1840s, Jewish settlement dates to the 1850s when individuals and families trickled into Minnesota Territory, attracted by mercantile and commercial opportunities opening up in the region, especially in St. Paul. Some arrived with savings or access to investment capital that enabled them to launch commercial careers. Clothing and dry-goods merchants predominated among them, although many started as peddlers. The Jewish population fluctuated depending on the economic health of the region.[6]

The first phase of Jewish group life in Minnesota was characterized by the middle-class status of members who lived within the context of the German cultural milieu. These newcomers grew in numbers and by 1856 were able

An early business in St. Paul was the Joseph Ullmann Fur Company, which was located at 353 Jackson St. when this picture was taken about 1875. Ullmann later sold the business to his cousins, and it then became the Rose Brothers Fur Company.

to establish the Mount Zion Hebrew congregation of St. Paul. This action signaled the beginnings of organized Jewish group life in Minnesota. Not all Jews in the territory joined Mount Zion, although for a time there were too few unaffiliated persons to organize other Jewish institutions. But in spite of the factionalism that plagued the congregation in its early years, everyone used the Mount Zion Cemetery, for burial in hallowed ground was a universal custom followed by even nonaffiliated Jews.[7]

Individuals from the early Jewish group participated without hindrance in Minnesota politics. During the territorial years from 1849 through 1857, Jacob Jackson Noah, son of a prominent New York Jacksonian Democrat, played a leading role. Arriving in St. Paul in 1849, he became an attorney and worked closely with such early political leaders as Henry H. Sibley and Alexander Ramsey. He was appointed clerk of the Dakota County District Court, and elected as the first clerk of the state Supreme Court in 1857. That same year Noah also served as secretary of the Democratic half of the Constitutional Convention. He was identified by his colleagues as a Jew, and he lectured on the history of the Jews to diverse audiences. Although Noah left the state after the Civil War, his activities inaugurated Jewish participation in the Minnesota political arena. Isaac Cardozo, descended from an illustrious Sephardic family and another Democrat, was appointed a deputy of the United States District Court in 1858. He was among the founders of Mount Zion and the first president of B'nai B'rith in Minnesota.[8]

After the Civil War, Jewish migration gathered momentum. Immigrants from Russia, Lithuania, and Poland were quickly absorbed into the framework of Jewish life in the state. Successful as peddlers, storekeepers, light manufacturers, and in licensed professions such as medicine, they nevertheless felt different from German Jews. By 1872 there were enough eastern Europeans in St. Paul to organize a separate religious congregation known as the Sons of Jacob. Neither distance nor belief separated German from eastern European Jew during this era; they lived near each other and subscribed to the same religious tenets. Rather it was language, social practices, and attitudes that divided the two groups.[9]

By 1875 the Jews of Minneapolis, which had become a thriving industrial town, were chastised by the *American Israelite*, a national newspaper, for their failure to found Jewish institutions and start a synagogue. A few months later the Montefiore Burial Society and *Baszion* (Daughter of Zion), a women's benevolent association, came into being. Practical necessity dictated the establishment of the burial society, for it was physically difficult to transport the dead to the St. Paul cemetery during the harsh winter months. Two years later in 1878 the Shaarai Tov congregation (later known as Temple Israel) was incorporated.[10]

Organized Jewish life was focused in the pioneer synagogues, and Mount Zion and Shaarai Tov remained the central institutions of the German settlers until the 1880s. Although small in size (as late as 1882 the membership of Mount Zion did not exceed 50 families), the synagogues spawned social and cultural subgroups that provided the communities with burial and charitable services. Embryonic educational activities for children were also begun.[11]

The existence of such separate institutions did not indicate that the German Jews were totally excluded from the state's general communal or political activities. This was particularly true in St. Paul, where they participated in such German cultural institutions as the *Turnverein*, a social and athletic club, and the *Sangverein*, a singing society, and contributed heavily to civic charities. Residential patterns, however, reinforced a tendency to cultivate their own institutions.[12]

As residents became more settled and successful in their economic life, rounds of entertainment, balls, and parties were held in their homes. Leisure-time pursuits moved away from the synagogues. Social clubs, discussion groups, and fraternal organizations began to play increasingly prominent roles for middle-class Jewish families in St. Paul and Minneapolis. Lodges of B'nai B'rith (Sons of the Covenant), a national, primarily German-Jewish fraternal organization founded in 1843, were established in St. Paul in 1871 and in Minneapolis in 1877. In addition, in 1875 St. Paul Jewish merchants organized the Standard Club as a place to make social and business contacts away from home and synagogue. Similarly Minneapolis, beginning in the early 1880s, had a series of short-lived social organizations, including the Apollo and two different Phoenix clubs.[13]

Economic success did not always result in social acceptance, as the spread of discrimination against German Jews in the eastern states showed. In Minnesota, however, few

VIEW IN MANNHEIMER BROTHERS' GREAT DRY GOODS ESTABLISHMENT, ST. PAUL.

Some dry-goods stores became full-fledged department stores, as did Mannheimer Brothers, 6th and Robert, St. Paul, which was once the largest in the Northwest. This engraving from *Northwest Magazine* was done in 1888.

such manifestations were recorded in the early years. On the contrary, a substantial number of affluent Jews seem to have married outside of the group or voluntarily disassociated from it, often by converting to other religious faiths.[14]

Such assimilationist conversions caused concern in the Minnesota community, but they were soon overshadowed by a more serious challenge—the unexpected arrival of large numbers of eastern European Jews, different in culture, appearance, and language, suffering from want, and challenging the western style of Judaism built up since the territorial years.

On Friday morning, July 14, 1882, just hours before the onset of the Jewish Sabbath, the community was shocked by the unannounced arrival at the St. Paul railroad depot of some 200 hungry, tired, dirty, and impoverished refugees from Russia. Men, women, and children, they taxed the philanthropic resources of the entire city.[15]

Emergency aid was quickly granted by Governor Lucius F. Hubbard, Mayor Edmund Rice, the city council, and the chamber of commerce. The refugees were fed, temporarily housed—first in the St. Paul, Minneapolis and Manitoba Railroad's immigrant house and then in a vacant school building—and welcomed amid the confusion. Within a few days they were settled in a temporary tent city on St. Paul's West Side, across the Mississippi River from the downtown district, in an area that was to become the main residence for subsequent eastern European Jewish settlers in St. Paul. Although not the first Russian-Jewish refugees to reach the state, this unannounced group awakened Minnesotans to the problems of absorbing refugees rather than immigrants.

A number of factors propelled these people from eastern Europe. Added to the rapidly disintegrating social and economic bases of Jewish life resulting from the early stages of modernization in Russia were the political and religious discriminations dictated by the czar and the

Russian Orthodox church. The Jews, designated as scape-goats to pacify increasing popular resentment against Czar Alexander II, were singled out for further persecution after revolutionaries assassinated him in March 1881. A series of laws promulgated in May of that year restricted Jewish residency rights, limited the geographical extent of the Pale of Settlement, and dispossessed large numbers of Jews from rural districts, compelling them to concentrate in already overcrowded villages in the western provinces of the Russian Empire. Economic and residential dislocation was followed rapidly by governmentally stimulated attacks. These pogroms hastened the decisions of many to flee. By the spring and summer of 1882 a mass exodus to western Europe was under way.

Fear that this influx would upset the delicate balance of Jewish intergroup relations on the continent and in England prompted efforts to divert the refugees across the Atlantic. In England the Mansion House Committee of London was formed to offer aid and to ensure that the refugees would not inundate the island. The work of the committee, in uneasy alliance with the Hebrew Emigrant Aid Society of New York, led in part to the shipment of the unannounced group that reached Minnesota.[16]

The hysterical exodus of the summer of 1882 subsided, but the patterns of Jewish settlement in the nation and the state were drastically altered. Chain migration resulted in a sustained flow of people to the New World. Continued repressive actions, pogroms, and social or economic dislocations periodically heightened the incoming levels. Only economic depression or war disrupted or slowed the movement.[17]

Before 1882 the entire Jewish population of the United States did not exceed 250,000. From that year until 1924, 3,000,000 to 4,000,000 arrived from eastern Europe. This pattern in microcosm can be traced in Minnesota. It is estimated that there were fewer than 1,000 Jews in the state prior to the 1880s. By the 1920s, when immigration quotas slowed the flow, some 30,000 to 40,000 Jews resided there.[18]

The year 1882 saw some 600 Jewish refugees settle in Minnesota, a number almost equal to the old-time, well-established Germanic element. The result was the evolution of a second distinct Jewish group composed of laborers and charity clients who were Yiddish speaking and more traditional in custom and outlook. The two communities lived in symbiotic relationship, sometimes exhibiting cooperative characteristics, but more often remaining at arm's length and displaying quiet hostility.[19]

The newcomers were perceived as a burden and as a potential threat by settled Jews. The St. Paul group fulfilled its charitable obligations without stint, while continuing to regard the newcomers as uneducated and thus backward dependents who must be "elevate[d] to a higher place." Fearful that such large numbers of refugees would swamp the local community, St. Paul Jews, like those in England, New York City, and Cincinnati, attempted to restrict the flow or divert it into other channels.[20]

One proposed alternative was to stimulate the settlement of Jewish migrants on the land. In Europe agriculture was increasingly viewed as the way to regularize and modernize the Jewish occupational pyramid. It was held that the absence of Jewish agrarians created a void that was a major source of social dislocation and anti-Jewish prejudice. The legal prohibition against Jewish farming in Russia was seen as a major cause for dispersion. Hence it was reasoned that the Russian exodus could be transformed into an opportunity to right a major occupational and social wrong. This thinking motivated the actions of several western European Jewish organizations and stimulated philanthropist Baron Maurice de Hirsch of Germany to create an international fund to assist in the establishment of a class of Jewish farmers in Palestine, Argentina, and the United States.[21]

In St. Paul, Rabbi Judah Wechsler of Mount Zion Temple agreed to sponsor the establishment of a Jewish agricultural settlement in Burleigh County, Dakota Territory, near Painted Woods on the Missouri River. He appears to have followed the advice of the Hebrew Emigrant Aid Society, which commissioned one of its members to study the possibilities of colonizing Russian refugees in the "West." During April and May 1882, Julius Goldman visited Minnesota and Dakota Territory, consulted with Roman Catholic Bishop John Ireland, personally inspected a number of possible agricultural sites, and wrote a report on his findings. He concluded that colonization on homestead or railroad lands was feasible, that it should be organized on an individual rather than a communal basis, and that the endeavor should be based upon business rather than charitable considerations.[22]

The belief that agriculture was the economic road to social salvation for the Jewish people led to a short-lived settlement in Minnesota. Early in 1891 Jacob H. Schiff, a New York investment banker active in Jewish affairs, attempted to establish an agricultural settlement at Milaca in Mille Lacs County. A long correspondence with James J. Hill resulted in the leasing of Great Northern Railroad lands for this endeavor. Apparently both men believed that a community situated on a railroad line and close to the Twin Cities would succeed. Schiff, with the permission of the Baron de Hirsch Fund, guaranteed that each family sent to Minnesota would have $500 to $600 in cash. Hill in turn completed arrangements to build 40 or 50 houses, each on 40 acres. Before the severe depression of 1893 made such ventures especially risky, a number of Jewish families were placed in the area. By 1898, however, only 13 families had been settled, and their fate is not known.[23]

By 1910 the Jewish Agricultural and Industrial Aid Society (JAIAS) counted only 13 agricultural families in the state. The dilemma of Jewish farming in Minnesota was that communal agriculture failed, yet the cultural, religious, and social needs of Jewish life required a population core unattainable under conditions of individualized, dispersed agriculture.[24]

In 1901 the JAIAS created yet another entity—the Industrial Removal Office (IRO)—to resettle immigrants from the overcrowded seaport cities to cities in the interior. The motives of the IRO were manifold—to prevent embarrassment to New York's successful German Jews, to spread out the burden of providing services to the newcomers, to reduce overcrowding, to reunite families, to provide greater economic opportunities to the immigrants, and to Americanize them more quickly. Traveling agents of the IRO in consultation with well-established Jews assessed the job capacities in each city they visited. Thereafter, once the immigrants were provided with railroad tickets, members of either B'nai B'rith or their wives, working through the local synagogue ladies benevolent societies, were enlisted to find them jobs and housing. Between 1901 and 1913, the IRO sent 2,250 to the state. Of that number, 75% were Russian, 14% Romanian, and the rest mixed. Minneapolis received 56% and St. Paul 31%. The remainder were sent to smaller towns.[25]

Realizing that the stream of people would be best diverted from the East Coast by providing other ports of entry, Jacob Schiff, between 1907 and 1913, funded an even-more restricted form of immigration. Through the so-called Galveston Project, his agents recruited mainly male skilled workers in Russia and paid for their passage to the port of Galveston and on by railroad to inland cities where, again, members of B'nai B'rith helped to settle them. While the project settled about 10,000 nationally, it probably did not add more than a few hundred to Minnesota's Jewish population. Instead chain migration (family members already in America sending for members in Europe) was responsible for the swelling population.[26]

City Life

By the beginning of the 20th century most Jewish immigrants lived in urban centers to which they had been attracted by job opportunities and by the well-established networks of religious, cultural, fraternal, and philanthropic institutions. By 1900 St. Paul alone had developed three major Jewish residential areas with a total population of 4,450–5,000. The older, more prestigious, and largely German families lived in the downtown area and on the bluffs overlooking the state capitol; some had begun to make inroads in the Summit Avenue neighborhood. Eastern Europeans—mainly small merchants, peddlers, and factory workers in the developing garment trades of the city—resided in two areas—east of the state capitol and on the West Side river flats. With increasing economic success they began moving across the Mississippi River and up the bluffs to the Selby-Dale neighborhood.[27]

Paralleling the rapid population growth of Minneapolis, Jewish areas there began to exceed the size of those in St. Paul. By 1900 approximately 5,000 Jews lived in Minneapolis, an increase of 4,500 since 1880. Although the economic and cultural gap between the German and the eastern European Jews was not as wide as that in St. Paul, distinct residential districts nevertheless developed.[28]

The earliest arrivals centered in the downtown area close to their businesses and to their synagogue, Temple Israel, which from 1888 until 1928 was located at 10th Street and 5th Avenue South. Newer arrivals from Romania and the Russian Empire concentrated in two separate neighborhoods, the Romanians on the South Side near the intersection of Franklin Avenue and 15th Street South and the Russians, Poles, and Lithuanians on the near North Side. The first area of settlement was in the vicinity of Washington Avenue and Fifth Street, the next had its religious-commercial nexus at Sixth Avenue North (later renamed Olson Highway) and Lyndale.[29]

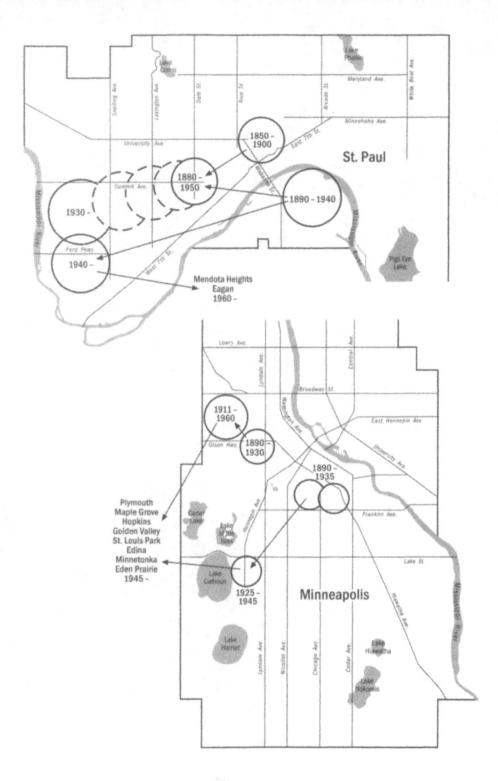

Jewish Neighborhoods in the Twin Cities, 1860–2000

Synagogue styles are not fixed. Temple Israel's Moorish structure built in 1890 harked back to the golden age of Spanish Jewry to which the Reform movement felt itself to be heir.

The South Side remained relatively stable until the 1940s as a self-contained family neighborhood. Residents lived near their jobs or businesses and were not pressured by other ethnic groups competing for housing. Those living on the North Side continued, between 1920 and 1940, to move in a north and west direction, a consequence of economic improvement and pressures from the growing Black population. While the third commercial hub centered on Plymouth Avenue particularly between Knox and

Kenesseth Israel Orthodox Synagogue, an immigrant synagogue, which was built about 1900 in Minneapolis, recalls the Russian Orthodox onion domes its builders were familiar with in Eastern Europe. By 1934 the building at 519 4th St. N. was no longer used as a place of worship.

Immigrant housing in the Twin Cities never approached the density of the lower East Side of New York, as this 1908 tenement scene on Minneapolis's North Side at 6th and Lyndale attests.

Upton Avenues, Jews remained within walking distance of the older area, where many synagogues and Jewish institutions remained. The newer neighborhood had a variety of housing, such as small bungalows and duplexes, as well as the upper-middle class Homewood area. Through World War II this section had the heaviest concentration of Jews in Minneapolis.[30]

In Duluth, where individual Jews had appeared as early as 1869, a range of organizations did not emerge until the city itself became a viable business center after the opening of the Mesabi Iron Range in the 1890s. The earliest arrivals, fairly Americanized Jews from the eastern United States, established businesses and bought houses in the affluent area east of Lake Avenue. Decades later the eastern European laborers settled in the city's West End, many of them renting low-cost housing between 12th and 24th Avenues. Never numerous, Duluth Jews totaled at their height in the 1930s about 4,000 people. Although they exhibited the same demographic split—an older German and a newer eastern European component—the arrival of one within a decade of the other precluded the wide divisions that characterized the St. Paul and, to a lesser extent, the Minneapolis experience. By 1900 Duluth had four synagogues. Organized

Male members of Adas Israel Synagogue, Duluth, gathered in 1919 on the bima at the front of the sanctuary before the beautiful two-story wooden ark, where the Torah scrolls are stored. The initial words of the Ten Commandments appear on the tablets at the top of the ark.

Jewish communities with religious, educational, philanthropic, and cultural institutions also emerged in the range cities of Hibbing, Eveleth, Virginia, and Chisholm. Although populations on the Mesabi fluctuated with the rise and decline of the iron ore industry, Jews continued to live in these northern Minnesota cities in the 1990s.[31] While Jewish communities also existed in Mankato, Austin, Albert Lea, and Rochester, only the last continued to have enough Jews to maintain a synagogue and rabbi.[32]

In larger cities the neighborhoods reflected the economic circumstances of the residents. Eastern Europeans who continued to settle in the state in large numbers during the first 15 years of the 20th century at first lacked the capital resources to follow the patterns of the well-established earlier arrivals. Carpenters, tailors, shoe repairmen, and other craftsmen often set up workshops in

their homes; dwellings frequently had junkyards located behind them; butchers, bakers, and grocers opened small shops nearby. Their wives took in boarders, and their daughters sewed in factories or clerked in stores. Butchers in particular were in demand because of the kosher dietary laws almost universally followed by their neighbors. Some immigrants without craft skills acquired them to become "Columbus' Tailors" in the New World.[33]

Many Jews with some knowledge of trading practices learned in their eastern European villages attempted to eke out a livelihood peddling. Although neither Minneapolis nor St. Paul reproduced the pushcart jungles of New York, many hawkers of fruits, vegetables, dry goods, pins, needles, and other cheap commodities were to be found. Some who were able to purchase or hire a horse and buggy expanded their routes beyond the Jewish neighborhoods.[34]

Peddling became widespread throughout the state, and many a hawker settled down as a retail merchant in one of the smaller market towns. Morris Kaplan of Bemidji, for example, began his career that way. He opened a general store there in 1908, built the Kaplan Glass Block in 1910, participated in the city's political and economic life, and

Tailoring, like peddling, was an eastern European Jewish specialty. In 1917 Simon Schwartz (with measuring tape) and his wife, Sadie, operated a tailor shop in St. Paul.

Eastern European Jews often started off peddling with a horse and wagon. Harry and David Silverman of St. Paul sold fruit from their wagon about 1920.

became active in the state's Socialist Party, running for Minnesota's United States Senate seat in 1934. Leon Salet, perhaps a more typical example, peddled his way from Winnipeg to Mankato in the early 1890s, where he was finally able, in 1896, to open a store. He brought over *landsleit* (people from his native shtetl) to help run the store and in time helped them to purchase stores in nearby towns, where he acted as their wholesaler. Desiring a richer Jewish life he left the store in the care of his sons in 1917 and moved to St. Paul, where he was prominent as a Jewish philanthropist.[35]

Few if any Jewish Minnesotans were to be found in such major economic endeavors as iron mining or flour milling, but a handful became grain merchants. Others followed the paths of their New York and Boston counterparts, pioneering as proprietors and entrepreneurs in the manufacture of specialty apparel such as furs and other types of winter clothing. Banking in the state was closed to Jews, as was the lumber industry. Employment in garment and cigar factories did not become widespread until a core of Jewish employers was established in the early 1900s, thus allowing Orthodox employees to follow their religious practices by closing on Saturdays and on Jewish holidays.[36]

Institutions and Organizations

Despite regional, cultural, and class differences, for most Jews the synagogue remained the central institution of their communal life. It was not only a place to worship and study the Torah (the Five Books of Moses) and the Talmud (scholarly commentaries), but also a major social institution and a home away from home, especially for the eastern Europeans. These immigrants attempted to reproduce as closely as possible the Old World practices they had known. Twice daily worship services, strict adherence to dietary laws, sharp physical separation of the sexes in the synagogue, complete abstinence from labor on the Sabbath, rigid adherence to all religious laws, firm following of the family practices during holidays, religious instruction in Hebrew for male children, ritual baths for women, daily

The family gathered on the front porch to celebrate the bris of Phillip Cohen, who is not present in the picture, in 1908 in Eveleth. The bris, or brit milah in Hebrew, is the covenantally mandated circumcision performed on each male child on the eighth day.

Bat mitzvah of Linda Grossman at Adath Jeshurun Synagogue, Minneapolis, 1954, with Rabbi Stanley Rabinowitz and Cantor Morris Amsel. The bar (for male) and bat (for female) mitzvah denotes the passage into the adult Jewish community and involves chanting parts of the Torah or the prophetic readings.

Wedding of Mel Zuckman and Clarice Sherman, Tifereth B'nai Jacob Synagogue, Minneapolis, 1951. At a Jewish wedding, the bride and groom stand under a chuppah or wedding canopy symbolizing their future home.

study of the Talmud—all this was conducted under the guidance of a learned rabbi who was both teacher and interpreter of the laws. The rigid requirements of Jewish law, followed meticulously by Orthodox Jews, the desire to worship with people from the same European country or locality, as well as regional variations in practices and customs produced a proliferation of synagogues located within the various Jewish residential areas of the Twin Cities. St. Paul alone had eight congregations, founded between 1872 and 1900. In Minneapolis 11 Orthodox synagogues were formed from 1884 to 1905. These *landsman* congregations were to be found primarily in the early phases of the immigrant experience. By the first decade of the 20th century, Old World geography was no longer a viable organizing principle for local synagogues.[37]

Because they were a minority group subject to the pressures of the surrounding society, many Jews gradually modified their traditional practices, but institutional forms were much slower to change. As long as Jews remained in the compact geographical areas where they were a dominant majority, they continued to attend Orthodox synagogues while moving away from the strict requirements as individuals. American secular life increasingly challenged the rigid traditionalism of Orthodox Judaism; the outcome was the creation of a national network of Reform (or Liberal) congregations in 1875, with a rabbinical school in Cincinnati. The liberal theologians worked out an ideology of intellectual and theological justification for Reform Judaism, culminating in a formally adopted outlook, which

The Torah is the repository of Jewish teachings and is accorded enormous respect. The scrolls are clad with richly embroidered coverings, and the wooden handles are covered with crowns or other decorations. Breastplates, similar to those worn by the High Priest, often adorn the front of the Torah. Jacob Langman, Michael Dorr, H. E. Gekler, and Ben Baugarten at the dedication of Beth Israel Hebrew Congregation, St. Paul, 1957.

Sukkot commemorates the fall harvest. It is celebrated by building sukkahs, temporary structures to eat in that are decorated with boughs and harvest fruits and vegetables. This sukkah was designed by Lucianne Hudak as part of a 1999 partnership project between the Minneapolis Institute of Arts and Rimon, the Jewish Metropolitan Council of Arts and Culture, an initiative of the Minneapolis Jewish Federation.

Z. Willard Finberg holding the shofar or ram's horn as he prepares for the High Holidays at Mount Zion in the 1950s. The shofar is blown several times during the Rosh Hashanah (New Year) service and at the end of Yom Kippur (Day of Atonement). The sound of the shofar is a call for self-reflection and repentance.

rejected the concepts of Jewish nationhood and ethnic and cultural distinctiveness for Jews in America. Following the western European, German, and British examples, it postulated the Jew as an American of the Hebrew faith. This new philosophy conformed perfectly to the disposition of the older German Jews, particularly in St. Paul and to a lesser extent in Minneapolis. Mount Zion Temple embraced the Reform ideology enthusiastically with the women in the forefront. In 1871 they asked permission for funds they had collected to be used for purchasing an organ, an instrument hitherto associated with the church.[38]

Ritual and theological changes further dramatized the separation of the German and eastern European Jewish groups, and physical removal from the immigrant neighborhoods completed the separation process. Between 1900 and 1910 most members of the older immigrant community moved from St. Paul's downtown to the Hill District, and in 1903 Mount Zion followed, constructing a new building at Holly and Avon Avenues near prestigious St. Paul churches. A new rabbi emphasized nontraditional elements of religious practice and even moved to Sunday services in conformity with Christian neighbors.[39]

Temple Israel, the Reform congregation in Minneapolis, avoided the theological and ritual extremes experi-

Members of the Burstein, Ravitzky, and Adelman families gathered for a seder meal in St. Paul in April 1943. This Passover meal begins with a retelling of the story of deliverance from Egyptian bondage and includes foods symbolic of the years of slavery and the flight from Egypt.

enced in St. Paul. Although it exhibited tendencies to liberal practices as early as 1880 and adopted the Reform prayer book in 1894, there was no sharp conflict with the Orthodox community for several reasons. The temple and its members were physically separated from the newer immigrants, and they had accepted Reform practices and ideas before the mass arrival of the eastern Europeans. Moreover Minneapolis lacked St. Paul's long tradition of German-Jewish integration into the wider community, a fact that was to have considerable bearing on the city's attitudes toward Jews in general. Still another important reason was the presence of Samuel N. Deinard, the rabbi appointed in 1901 to serve Temple Israel, who was a moderate reformer, a Zionist at a time when Reform Judaism was anti-Zionist, and a conciliator. Throughout his 20-year career, he sought to bridge the gap between his congregants and the Yiddish-speaking Jews of the community.[40]

The Reform ideology of Judaism did not, however,

Rabbi Samuel Deinard ministered to Temple Israel congregants until his death in 1921. He was also the founder of the weekly *American Jewish World*.

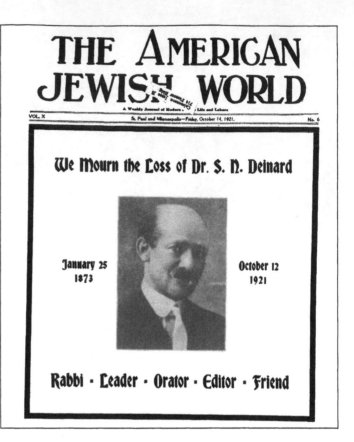

THE AMERICAN JEWISH WORLD

A Weekly Journal of Modern Jewish Life and Labors

VOL. X   St. Paul and Minneapolis—Friday, October 14, 1921.   No. 6

We Mourn the Loss of Dr. S. N. Deinard

January 25
1873

October 12
1921

Rabbi · Leader · Orator · Editor · Friend

attract all those who sought an accommodation between Jewish practices and modern needs. For some, a third alternative was to be found in Conservative Judaism, a movement that emerged nationally in the first decade of the 20th century with the founding of the Jewish Theological Seminary in New York City. Its efforts were directed toward conserving traditional Judaism while modifying it to meet modern conditions.[41]

In Minneapolis Adath Jeshurun, a South Side Orthodox congregation, moved into the Conservative camp as early as 1907, and a group of young people who had grown up on the North Side and been educated at the Talmud Torah started Beth El in 1921. In St. Paul the Temple of Aaron emerged from a congregation organized in 1910. When a new building, erected at Ashland and Grotto in the Hill District, was opened in 1916, the congregation chose a graduate of the Jewish Theological Seminary as spiritual leader.

Despite the inroads of Reform and Conservative ideologies, Orthodox synagogues continued to proliferate. In Minneapolis two on the North Side merged to form Kenesseth Israel in 1891. The maturity and stability of the local community were demonstrated by the dedication of a new synagogue building during the depths of the de-

Architect Jack Liebenberg designed a moderne structure for Beth El Synagogue at 1349 Penn Ave. N. on the North Side in 1926. It reflected his sensibility as well as this Conservative synagogue's more modern approach to Jewish worship.

pression of 1893. Kenesseth Israel became the most influential Orthodox congregation in the city and was still thriving at the turn of the next century. After 1900 four additional Orthodox synagogues on the North Side and three on the South Side continued to serve the growing eastern European population of Minneapolis. Similarly in St. Paul at least four new congregations were established after 1900.[42]

The steady erosion of membership in Orthodox synagogues, however, compelled a modest modernization effort both nationally and locally. Kenesseth Israel in Minneapolis and Sons of Jacob in St. Paul increased the use of English in services, hired rabbis trained in America, and encouraged the involvement of their leaders in the nonreligious aspects of Jewish and American communal life. By the 1950s, Sons of Jacob and Mikro Kodesh even allowed women to sit in a section on the first floor instead of in the customary balcony. Nonetheless, the laws and practices of Orthodoxy made retention of adherents increasingly difficult. For example, as Jews dispersed to the suburbs west of Minneapolis and south of St. Paul, distances were too great to walk to the synagogues, yet auto travel was precluded by the Orthodox admonition not to ride on the Sabbath or holy days.

Dramatic changes also took place in Reform congregations after 1940. Attracted by the greater freedom of Reform practices and the overt commitment to the wider community and to broad social justice, large numbers of the children and grandchildren of eastern European immigrants joined Temple Israel and Mount Zion. In the process, more traditional elements found their way into the congregations, softening the sharp edge of Reform with increased use of Hebrew, a greater appreciation of Yiddish, a general acceptance of the concept of the Jews as a nation rather than merely a religious group, the reinstitution of Bar Mitzvah and the introduction of Bat Mitzvah ceremonies, and the inclusion of Jewish cultural content in temple programs.[43]

The absence of large numbers of Jews outside the Twin Cities precluded similar institutional religious developments elsewhere. In the smaller communities the divisions were not as wide and compromise usually moved the congregation into the Conservative mode. Only Duluth had enough Jewish families to enable differentiation. In 1945 Tifereth Israel changed from Orthodox to Conservative; in

Mount Zion Congregation selected Erich Mendelsohn, a noted German-trained architect, for its Summit Avenue temple, which was finished in 1954.

1970 it merged with the Reform Temple Emanuel to create a new congregation, Temple Israel. By 1973 only one Orthodox synagogue, Adas Israel, remained.[44]

The proliferation of organizations has been a characteristic of Jewish communities throughout the United States, and those in Minnesota were no exception. Jews in the state enthusiastically embraced the principle of voluntary association, founding a bewildering array of fraternal, charitable, cultural, political, and religious groups. Philanthropy became a key ingredient of the voluntary organizations spun off from the pioneer temples, and self-help dominated their philosophies.

The Hebrew Ladies Benevolent Society (HLBS), for example, organized by prominent members of Mount Zion in 1871, raised money to help indigent Jews by holding bake sales, strawberry festivals, and charity balls. When eastern European immigrants arrived, the HLBS took upon themselves the task of "friendly visiting" in order to ascertain whether newcomers were truly destitute and worthy of receiving assistance. They provided coal, new eyeglasses, payment of hospital bills, and even train fare to other cities. The Baszion Society in Minneapolis (renamed the HLBS in 1880 and the Temple Israel Auxiliary in 1903) and

Duluth's Temple Emanuel's auxiliary served a similar function. All helped to furnish their synagogues, pay off mortgages, provide parties for Sunday School children, and aid poorer members of the Jewish community.[45]

Not content with being passive recipients of charity, eastern European Jews set up their own constellation of voluntary organizations. The Sisters of Peace Benevolent Society was created in 1882 as the Orthodox equivalent of Mount Zion's HLBS. It and the Charity Loan Society, founded in 1890, combined forces to establish the Jewish Home for Aged in 1906. Its first president, Mary Burton, in 1908 persuaded men to become involved because a home had been purchased and the women became worried about the cost of maintaining the inmates. A year later, the board was entirely male, and a female president was not elected again until the late 1970s. In St. Paul, the Daughters of Abraham founded Sholom Home, a chronic care facility, which in 1971 merged with the Jewish Home for the Aged.[46]

Whether they were called ladies aid societies, women's auxiliaries, or synagogue sisterhoods, the task was the same—raising funds for the institution, beautifying it, and taking care of members. These women of the Sunshine Club of Virginia in 1909 visited the sick and cheered up the housebound.

The ever-increasing demands of local, national, and international philanthropic groups and their apparent duplications and inefficiencies led to an effort to consolidate such endeavors in the Twin Cities. The United Jewish Charities of St. Paul, which incorporated in 1910, had as its founders Mount Zion's Jewish Relief Society and the Orthodox community's Sisters of Peace, Bickur

Ada Rubenstein, the first woman to be president of Sholom Home, St. Paul, joined resident Ida Gepner at groundbreaking ceremonies for a new building in the late 1970s.

Cholim Society, and the Hebrew Ladies Aid Society. By 1920 it was renamed the Jewish Welfare Association. A similar evolution occurred in Minneapolis where in 1880 Temple Israel's HLBS and the Sisters of Peace, an Orthodox group, formed United Hebrew Charities. Thirty years later, these two merged with the Jewish Loan Society, the B'nai B'rith Free Employment Bureau, the Sheltering Home for Transients, and the Jewish Free Dispensary to become the Associated Jewish Charities of Minneapolis. Professionalization of social welfare services emerged after 1915. By 1918 the Minneapolis organization was so well

The Jewish Sheltering Home, a short-term care facility, was located in North Minneapolis. In the center of this group in 1925 is "Mother" Farbstein, who was superintendent for many years.

The St. Paul Hebrew Institute offered religious instruction to youngsters upstairs in this building at 295 Kentucky, about 1940. The Shelter House downstairs provided simple sleeping accommodations for Jewish travelers. Furnishing hospitality to wayfarers is a time-hallowed Jewish injunction.

accepted that the local War Chest, and its successor the Community Fund, invited the Associated Charities to participate in the city's consolidated fund drive.[47]

During this period the focus of Jewish charitable activities shifted from integrating the immigrant into the community to dealing with the indigent and problem families. Reflecting the new emphasis, the Associated Jewish Charities name was changed to the Jewish Family Welfare Association in 1924 and in 1946 to the Jewish Family Service Association and later the Jewish Family and Children's Service. Whatever its name, however, this organization served as the primary social welfare agency of the Minneapolis Jewish community. Similar groups were active in St. Paul and Duluth. By the time the Great Depression descended on the nation in the 1930s, these agencies were engaged in multifaceted casework rather than merely in direct relief.[48]

Regardless of the efforts of the Jewish Family Welfare Association, educational, social, political, and international relief organizations continued to proliferate. By 1936 some 94 separate organizations existed in Minneapolis alone, with St. Paul and Duluth not far behind in the variety and diversity of organized groups. The idea of combining fund raising for all groups into one effort had long been advocated by professional workers, but it was not until 1930 that the Minneapolis Federation for Jewish Service was incorporated. Successfully directed by an executive board and coordinated by a small professional staff, the Federation endured in 2001 as the principal organization planning for the community's future, raising the needed funds, and integrating the work of numerous Jewish agencies in Minneapolis. In St. Paul the United Jewish Fund and Council performed a similar function. Duluth had the Northland Jewish Fund until 2001.[49]

For all the formation of umbrella organizations, those with a single mission continued to multiply. Benefit societies, some affiliated with national organizations and in many cases purely local, developed as a preferred means of self-help for Minnesota Jews. The fraternal benefit groups collected small monthly payments, insured members' lives, and in some cases provided a primitive form of prepaid health benefits. Emergency collections taken up at lodge meetings frequently supplemented these payments to sick or destitute fellow members. The most prominent of the self-help fraternal orders was B'rith Abraham (Covenant of Abraham), which at its peak prior to World War I enrolled a few thousand members in its lodges in Minneapolis, St. Paul, Duluth, and the iron range towns.[50]

The women's divisions of the St. Paul and Minneapolis Jewish Federations once covered the Jewish areas of the Twin Cities in one-day, well-planned campaigns. Since the 1950s, the fund-raising period has grown lengthier and the tactics more sophisticated.

Loan societies abounded as well. Some were associated with synagogues, as was Minneapolis' Gemilus Chesed Society, others with the Socialist Workmen's Circle, while a few groups were independent. Some charged interest; others did not. In St. Paul, for example, the Women's Free Loan Society, founded in 1915, provided immigrant women with seed money to furnish their homes or start a business.[51]

Relatively quickly, however, bridging institutions sought to promote communal integration. Early in the 20th century, B'nai B'rith opened its lodges to active and successful eastern European men, while their wives joined such organizations as the National Council of Jewish Women (NCJW). The latter, founded in Chicago in 1893, provided spiritual, educational, and philanthropic activities that would address the concerns of American Jewish women and campaigned for women's rights, including the right to vote.[52]

The Minneapolis section was established in 1894 by Nina Morais Cohen, who was present at the beginning of the national organization. This daughter of Sabato Morais, one of the founders of the Jewish Theological Seminary, and his wife, Clara, showed her intellectual gifts early and became a champion of woman suffrage. She married Emanuel Cohen, a lawyer, and they moved to Minneapolis in 1886. She hosted Susan B. Anthony and was a charter member of the Minneapolis Women's Club. Cohen invited immigrant women who showed promise as leaders to join her rigorous NCJW study sessions, thereby teaching them how to conduct research, write reports, and deliver speeches.[53]

Although the NCJW fostered eastern European women in leadership roles, it remained a bastion of Reform women until after World War II. An atypical exception was Fanny Fligelman Brin, who emigrated from Romania as a child in 1884 and who was a 1907 Phi Beta Kappa graduate of the University of Minnesota, joined the Minneapolis chapter, where she carried out her commitments to women's rights, world peace, and her Jewish heritage. From 1932 to 1938 Fanny Brin served as the ninth president of the national NCJW. In Minnesota she organized the Women's United Nations Rally in 1944 to promote peace and education.[54]

While education remained a prominent feature of the NCJW, it was their philanthropic efforts that gained them renown. In St. Paul concern for the values and economic well-being of Jewish youths prompted the founding of a settlement house on the West Side river flats in 1895. Neighborhood House, initially called the Industrial School, began as an effort of the NCJW and the HLBS of Mount Zion. It was intended to provide industrial training for Jewish immigrant children following the economic crisis of 1893. Rapidly expanding its services to meet additional needs, Neighborhood House was by 1897 a true social settlement, offering recreational as well as formal and informal educational opportunities.[55]

Even though it remained closely associated with the welfare initiatives of Mount Zion, the house was reorganized on a nonsectarian basis in 1903. After 1905 it employed professional workers to organize the clubs, day-care centers, and physical educational activities, which succeeded in luring immigrant youngsters off the streets. For two generations Neighborhood House helped reinforce Jewish values, despite the clash of cultures and the pressures of assimilation accompanying the Americanization drives during and following World War I. By World War II the ethnic composition of the West Side flats had changed, and Neighborhood House was serving primarily a Mexican clientele.

In the 1920s the Minneapolis section of NCJW followed St. Paul's example by establishing the South Side Neighborhood House. They also conducted a Sunday school for children on the North Side. The Emanuel Cohen Center, which emerged from the expanded activities of Talmud

Torah, served the Jews on the North Side. The second Talmud Torah building, located at 8th and Fremont Avenue North had contained recreation space, including a gym and swimming pool, as well as a social service department. Both outgrew their quarters, and in 1924 an older home in the Oak Lake area was purchased, remodeled, and named for the attorney who was its major benefactor. There it provided inexpensive health and dental care facilities. The center's primary role, however, was to offer an alternative to

The Emanuel Cohen Center served Jews who lived on the North Side of Minneapolis. In 1925 one activity of their social service department was running a well-baby clinic.

the street, a function it continued to play until the North Side Jewish community dispersed after the 1950s.[56]

While the settlement house provided one alternative to the lure of the street, the major threat to Jewish youth was to their cultural and religious survival. As in most immigrant communities, Jewish education in the Twin Cities was chaotic. Largely the work of old-fashioned itinerant teachers, whose use of rote-learning methods was resented by children, their tutelage failed to meet the heightened need for cultural survival. As a result, the Minneapolis Talmud Torah was founded to perpetuate Jewish learning in modern, secular, urban America. It opened in 1894 as the Hebrew Free School in a vacant butcher shop. Its evolution into a modern afternoon school, with a full curriculum of Jewish subjects from elementary through secondary levels, awaited the creative volunteer efforts of Dr. George J. Gordon, an immigrant from Lithuania who bridged the gap between traditionalism and modernism, medical science and the Jewish heritage. He introduced modern pedagogy, graded classes, and a rigorous curriculum in the new Talmud Torah that opened on Minneapolis' North Side in 1911.[57]

Within a few years, the school had become the Jewish community's dominant educational institution while remaining independent of any religious congregation. By

Sports played an important role in Americanizing immigrant groups, teaching them the so-called Anglo-Saxon virtue of fair play. The Minneapolis Talmud Torah, whose mission was teaching Hebrew language and Jewish customs, had an active alumni athletic association. In 1920 they produced this championship football team, one of whose members, Louis Gross, top center, went on to play for the University of Minnesota.

Although the Emanuel Cohen Center had no gym, it sponsored teams that practiced at other nearby settlement houses or in public schools. One such team was the Aurora Athletic Club in 1933.

1928 its educational reputation, which emphasized Hebrew as a spoken language, was worldwide, and Gordon gave up his medical practice to assume full-time direction. Even after a second and third generation replaced the immigrant children, its enrollment remained high. Talmud Torah expanded, set up branch schools on the South Side, and in the mid-20th century followed the Jewish population to the suburbs. Not until the period from 1965 to 1972 did the institution report a 35% decline in enrollment.

A Minneapolis parochial school, Torah Academy, was established in 1944 by a minority of Orthodox Jews who were dissatisfied with the Hebrew cultural emphasis of Talmud Torah and wanted to provide a total Jewish religious education for their children. Duluth had its own Talmud Torah, started by the redoubtable Ida Cook, but no comparable day school was created. Depending on the

Organized team sports under Jewish auspices remained popular, as shown here by members of Sons of Herzl AZA, a branch of the national B'nai B'rith Youth Organization network of clubs, in 1950.

Jewish density, iron range towns and Rochester provided afternoon or weekend schools.[58]

Dr. George Gordon taught at the precursor of the Minneapolis Talmud Torah in the 1890s. Talked out of becoming a rabbi, he earned a medical degree in 1900 and practiced on the North Side. He became director of the Talmud Torah in 1929 and died in 1943, two years after this picture was taken.

The story of Jewish education in St. Paul reflects denominational divisiveness as well as neighborhood autonomy. Sons of Jacob Congregation established a Hebrew school in Lowertown as early as 1881, which in 1912 became the Capitol City Hebrew Free School. A year earlier the Orthodox synagogues of the West Side together founded the St. Paul Hebrew Institute while the Temple of Aaron organized its own school in 1916. With the completion of a new community building in 1931, the latter school moved and became independent. It was renamed the St. Paul Talmud Torah in 1956 when it merged with the Capitol City school. It later moved to Highland Park where it continued to provide a cultural education while remaining unaffiliated with any synagogue.

As larger numbers of Jews began working downtown,

Children learned to write in Hebrew at the Jewish Education Center in St. Paul in 1931.

social clubs sprang up to meet their needs. In St. Paul the 19th-century Standard Club in time accepted eastern European Jews. Not until the 1920s when the St. Paul Athletic Club opened its doors to Jewish members did the Standard go out of existence. In Minneapolis the need for a downtown club was felt when it became apparent that existing city organizations were reluctant to enroll Jews. In addition, those moving from the older neighborhoods wished to remain in touch with their friends. In 1908 a group of University of Minnesota graduates founded the Gymal Daled Club, named for the third and fourth letters of the Hebrew alphabet. Primarily a social and athletic organization, it also served lunch and sponsored cultural events.[59] Other downtown clubs, such as the Atlas, Pro-North, and Ampliora, were by 1919 absorbed by Gymal Daled. With increasing acculturation, the members decided in 1945 to change its name to the Standard Club. This institution existed into the 1980s largely as a businessman's group, although in the 1970s such exclusive bastions as the Minneapolis Club and the Minneapolis Athletic Club began to welcome some prominent Jews into their ranks.[60]

Another cluster of organizations came into being to serve the large numbers of Jewish students who attended the University of Minnesota in Minneapolis. As early as 1904 a Jewish Literary Society began meeting regularly. In 1911 it joined the national Menorah (Enlightenment) Society, formed to help students cope with the coldness of campus life. By the 1920s Minnesotans had assumed positions of leadership in this national movement.[61] Through the dismal depression years of the 1930s, the students especially felt the absence of a Jewish center on campus, in part because of the rising tide of anti-Semitism at home and abroad. With support from the national B'nai B'rith and the Jewish communities of Minneapolis and St. Paul, Hillel House opened by 1944 and later moved into a new building constructed in 1956.[62]

The *American Jewish World*, Minnesota's sole Jewish newspaper, kept readers informed of local, national, and international events of Jewish concern, pointed out needed changes and reforms, and galvanized the community in times of crisis. Founded by Rabbi Samuel Deinard in June 1912, it was called the *Jewish Weekly* for its first three years. As editor, Deinard successfully involved other Jewish leaders in the work of the paper, consciously seeking to balance his editorial opinions with various viewpoints. In 2001 the *American Jewish World* was still widely read by Jews in Minnesota.[63]

Students and members of the community gathered for a ribbon cutting at Hillel House to celebrate its opening, about 1944.

Less successful was an attempt in 1921 to publish a Yiddish-language weekly. Although more than 13,000 foreign-born Minnesotans named Yiddish as their mother tongue in 1920, the *Shabbosdige Post* (Saturday or Sabbath Post), which first appeared on September 23, 1921, lasted only three years. During its final year of publication, its pages were evenly divided between Yiddish and English material. Several factors may have contributed to its failure: competing national Yiddish dailies were being published in New York, and Americanizing pressures dictated a move away from Yiddish. Thus the success of Deinard's English-language weekly and the failure of the Yiddish one might be interpreted as manifestations of the increased acculturation of Minnesota Jews.[64]

Politics: Actions and Reactions

Although always a distinct minority, nonreligious, politically active Jews were present in the Minnesota population from territorial times. In the early 20th century their numbers included a group that identified with Socialism, saw the salvation of the Jewish people in the attainment of a classless society, favored the use of Yiddish for cultural and artistic expression, and attempted to create institutions to serve its needs. Among the members were veterans of the revolutionary struggles in the Russian Empire who had belonged to the Jewish Socialist Workers Association of Russia, Poland, and Lithuania (the Bund). This group had broken with Lenin and the Bolsheviks after 1903 over the question of cultural autonomy, for it wished to maintain the use of Yiddish within the revolutionary movement. The failed Russian Revolution of 1905 compelled many members to seek asylum in the United States, where some found their way to Duluth, the North Side of Minneapolis, and the West Side of St. Paul.[65]

During the life of the first immigrant communities in these cities, Yiddish Socialists constituted a creative, but often disruptive, minority. They established a vibrant network of cultural, political, fraternal, and educational institutions and successfully attracted a number of second-generation followers. They formed clubs that affiliated with the Jewish Socialist Federation of the Socialist Party. Actively involved in the labor and political struggles of the Twin Cities, this group in 1916 helped elect Thomas Van Lear, the only Socialist mayor Minneapolis ever had.[66]

Self-help with a Socialist and Yiddish twist was the objective in forming the 1910 Minneapolis and St. Paul branches of the Workmen's Circle, a fraternal organization that provided medical and insurance benefits to members. The circles also organized Yiddish libraries, performed Yiddish plays, established Yiddish-language schools, and sponsored prominent Yiddish lecturers. A similar group in Duluth, founded in 1911, remained viable through the 1930s.[67]

Although the Bolshevik Revolution of 1917 in Russia caused a split within this movement, with one group eventually affiliating with the Communist Party and the other remaining in the Socialist camp, both wings remained dedicated to the perpetuation of Yiddish secularism with a

The Workmen's Circle, a national Jewish Socialist organization, had branches in St. Paul, Minneapolis, and Duluth. Delegates from these chapters gathered in 1918 for a regional meeting.

radical, anticapitalist orientation. In 1915, at the height of their influence, Yiddishist radicals built the Labor Lyceum as a nonreligious, social center on the Minneapolis North Side. But the movement gradually waned, a victim of acculturation. By the end of the 1940s, with the gradual disappearance of a Jewish proletariat, only a small remnant could still be found in the city.[68]

Over the years other events besides the Russian Revolutions affected the well-being of Jews in Europe and frequently concerned those in Minnesota. When political anti-Semitism emerged in western Europe at the end of the 19th century, the St. Paul Jewish community responded with protests and political actions. After the Dreyfus Affair in France in the 1890s, its protests were echoed by many non-Jewish Minnesota religious leaders. The massacres of Jews in Kishinev, Russia, in 1903 and the government-sponsored pogroms stimulated a rare unanimity among local Jews, who joined in relief activities abroad and political agitation at home in an attempt to persuade the United States to repudiate its trade agreement with Russia.[69]

After the outbreak of World War I in 1914, when Jews living in the battle zones between the Russian and German armies seemed to be in jeopardy, all factions of Minnesota Jewry again responded. Workers donated a day's wages to relieve the starving Russian Jewish masses, the left-wing People's Relief Committee raised funds among its Jewish adherents, and others participated in national campaigns directed by the American Jewish Committee and the Joint Distribution Committee.

Relief efforts during and immediately after World War I and following the Russian Revolution gave Minnesota's eastern European Jews opportunities to assume leadership positions. When alleged "undemocratic" control of international efforts by affluent Jews on the American Jewish Committee was challenged, and a more representative body known as the American Jewish Congress resulted, it was supported by large numbers of Minnesota Jews. The congress sought postwar guarantees of Jewish rights in the newly created European states. In this effort, however, it was to be disappointed.

The rise of Fascism and Nazism in the 1930s, with their threats to the very survival of European Jewry, drew mass protests from Minnesota Jews. When Hitler's government proclaimed the racist Nuremberg Laws in 1935, depriving German Jews of various rights and forbidding them to marry non-Jews, a small number of the state's Jewish leaders advised quiet diplomacy. A majority, however, opted for mass demonstrations, a boycott of German goods, and agitation for immigration of Jewish refugees from Germany to the United States. Fanny Brin and Charles Cooper, then executive director of the Minneapolis Jewish Family Welfare Association, formed the Minneapolis Refugee Service Committee and by the fall of 1940 had settled 250 European refugees in the city.[70]

Not until 1948 were Displaced Persons (DPs) permitted to enter the country. By 1952, 269 families, consisting of about 800 people, had settled in Minneapolis, 168 families (365 people) in St. Paul, 28 families in Duluth, and a smaller number in other parts of the state.[71] While the DPs were aided by the Jewish community, its members simply could not comprehend the experiences the refugees had undergone. One reason may have been the discomfort that America's Jews felt at not having done more once the presence of Hitler's death camps became common knowledge. There was, as well, a preoccupation with Israel's War of Independence. Still another factor was the wish to portray Jews not as victims but as brave pioneers and fierce fighters. It was not until the late 1960s that the former DPs were encouraged to relate their experiences.[72]

The revelation that between five and six million European Jews were exterminated by the Nazis during the 1940s did, however, have a profound and traumatic impact on American Jews. Shocked and guilt ridden that they had not been able to rescue their brothers and sisters, those in Minnesota resolved to react with greater vigilance to every threat to the survival of the Jewish people. A communal pledge that the Holocaust would never be repeated supplied a uniting force for the diverse elements of the state's Jewish communities.[73]

As a result, Zionism gained further support in Minnesota. The rise of the Zionist movement, which emphasized creating a Jewish homeland, uniting the Jewish people, and bringing about a Hebrew cultural renaissance, had attracted attention in the state during the decade preceding World War I. Zionism had long been a strong force in Minneapolis. Endorsed by Rabbi Samuel Deinard, the message was disseminated through the pages of the *American Jewish World* and preached from the pulpit of Temple Israel, much to the discomfort of temple members. Various strands of Zionism had long enjoyed the allegiance of numbers of eastern European Jews. The 1936 Jewish Communal Survey counted eleven such. Zionism was at first opposed by St. Paul's Reform religious leaders, by well-integrated German Jews, and by Socialists. The leadership provided by Louis C. Brandeis, who served as a United States Supreme Court Justice from 1916 to 1939, reassured German Jews that Zionism was not the divisive expression of disloyalty to the United States that they had at first thought.[74]

After the British proclamation of the Balfour Declaration in 1917 supporting Zionist objectives and the establishment of the Palestine Mandate by the League of Nations in 1922, Minnesota Zionists worked tirelessly to assist in the building of a Jewish national presence in Palestine. The most active group was Hadassah, the women's Zionist organization. Founded nationally in 1912 by Henrietta Szold, the St. Paul chapter was organized a year later and immediately had 79 members; Chisholm's chapter was founded in 1919, and Minneapolis' around that same time. Hadassah women worked tirelessly to support a visiting nurse program and build a hospital. During the 1930s, they transported Jewish youth from troubled spots in Europe to live in villages in Palestine.[75]

The Jewish National Fund, still another organization, attempted to purchase land in Palestine. In the 1930s Labor Zionists established a training farm north of Minneapolis in Champlin to prepare potential communal farmers for life on the kibbutz, but only a small number of Minnesota Jews emigrated to Palestine. Zionism remained a minority

Young Zionists worked on the Hachsharah farm in Anoka in the 1930s to prepare them for a farming future in Palestine/Israel.

movement in Minnesota with fewer than 2,500 members in its various organizations in 1920. Although it did not achieve majority status until after 1945, it was still a potent force for education and advocacy.[76]

Although most Minnesotans continued to be supporters from afar, the establishment of the state of Israel in 1948 brought forth a spontaneous celebratory demonstration as well as a massive fund drive. Arab military attacks on Israel in 1948, 1967, and 1973 resulted in extraordinary financial, political, and emotional efforts by Minnesota Jewish groups. Annual fund drives conducted by the Jewish Federations in the Twin Cities raised money to support institutions in Israel. Minnesota Jews bought bonds and contributed to the Jewish National Fund, Hadassah Hospital, Hebrew University, and social service agencies working to integrate Jews from Europe and the Arab countries into the new state. Thus events accomplished a redefinition of Zionism. For most Minnesota Jews, it came to mean support for Israel's survival and identification with its aspirations through institutional ties with the Jewish homeland.[77]

Anti-Semitism was not only an issue abroad. Jews in Minneapolis faced it every day. Whereas nationally a career in teaching was becoming a route for educated second-generation Jews for upward mobility, few were so employed in Minneapolis. Jews were also conspicuous by their absence as employees of major Minneapolis retail,

banking, and manufacturing establishments. Similar patterns of discrimination were discernible to a lesser degree
in other parts of the state. But it was the successful use of
anti-Semitism as a political weapon during the 1930s that
caused Minnesota Jews to organize countermeasures. Coin-
ciding with the rise of Nazism, numerous Fascist political
groups acquired recruits in the state. Particularly successful were the Silver Shirts and Father Charles Coughlin's Social Justice movement. By calling attention to the fact that
some Jews were prominent supporters of Governors Floyd
B. Olson and Elmer A. Benson of the Farmer-Labor Party
and that a number held jobs in state agencies and the governor's office, these groups attempted to equate Jewishness
with radicalism and Communism.[78]

Although such propaganda was not overwhelmingly
successful, some elements among Minnesota's old economic and political elites used the same tactics to discredit
and defeat the Farmer-Labor administration. Anti-Semitic
whispering campaigns, posters, and pamphlets were used
by Ray P. Chase and one segment of the Republican Party

Campers sitting on the porch roof of a building at Herzl Camp, Webster, Wisconsin, about 1990. The camp serves Jewish teens from all over the Midwest, teaching them Hebrew and inculcating them with a love of Israel. The camp was named for Theodore Herzl, the founder of modern Zionism, whose silhouette is seen on the sign along with his famous statement, "If you will it, it is no dream."

to defeat Elmer Benson's re-election efforts in the 1938 race for governor. The participation of Jewish trade unionists Sander D. Genis, Rubin Latz, and Michael L. Finkelstein in the industrial union organizing drives of the 1930s gave anti-Semites further reasons to raise funds from leading Minnesota banks and companies to end Farmer-Labor domination of the state's executive branch. Their efforts were successful. After Benson was defeated, Republicans occupied the Minnesota governorship until 1955.

In response the Minnesota Jewish Council came into being as an investigative, lobbying, and educational agency. Under the energetic leadership of Samuel L. Scheiner, its executive director during 1939–44, 1946–51, and 1953–74, the council worked to combat anti-Semitism. Little progress was achieved, however, until after national attention spotlighted the Minneapolis situation.[79]

In the fall of 1946 Minnesotans were disturbed to find Minneapolis described by the noted journalist Carey McWilliams as "the capital of anti-Semitism in the United States." Jews were not surprised, for they had long lived with job discrimination, housing restriction, stereotyped views, hostility, and other manifestations of anti-Jewish sentiment. Late in the 19th century anti-Semitism had found expression in *Caesar's Column*, a novel by Minnesota Populist leader Ignatius Donnelly, which characterized Jewish middlemen as social enemies. Expressions of anti-Semitism in the 20th century spewed from the pulpits of such popular Minneapolis evangelists as William Bell Riley and Luke Rader. Social discrimination was manifested by the inability of Jews to gain membership in many local groups. Jewish country clubs, like Oak Ridge in Minneapolis and Hillcrest in St. Paul, had been started in the

1920s because existing clubs were closed to them. As late as 1948 Jews were denied membership in the Minneapolis Automobile Association, the Minneapolis Athletic Club, the Kiwanis, Rotary, Lions, and similar organizations. They could not buy homes in certain sections of Minneapolis, and Jewish real estate salesmen were excluded from the local realty board. Jewish physicians had difficulty acquiring hospital privileges.[80]

Jay Phillips was a noted philanthropist and one of the founders of Mount Sinai Hospital. He and his wife, Rose, attended the Mount Sinai Ball in 1980.

These affronts prompted Minneapolis Jewish community leaders to act upon a study done in 1944 to determine the feasibility of constructing a Jewish hospital in Minneapolis. After many setbacks, Mount Sinai Hospital opened its doors in 1951, proudly proclaiming itself a "non-sectarian facility." The hospital provided Minneapolis with much needed beds and Jewish doctors with a superb facility in which to care for their patients. Not coincidentally, it enhanced the prestige of Jewish business leaders who, with the change of political climate, were soon invited to serve on civic boards.[81]

The McWilliams article galvanized Minneapolis' political-civic power structure. Coming so soon after the nation was repelled by the revelations of Jewish genocide in Europe, the 1946 pronouncement forced Minneapolitans to recognize that only a narrow line separated racial prejudice from genocide. Elected in 1945, Mayor Hubert H. Humphrey headed a new city administration that undertook to eliminate this blot on Minneapolis' reputation. Humphrey appointed a blue-ribbon Mayor's Council on Human Relations, which surveyed the local situation and, in the course of the years from 1946 to 1949, proposed ordinances to ensure civil rights and discourage housing and job discrimination. On the state level, Republican Governors Edward J. Thye and Luther W. Youngdahl sponsored measures to outlaw discrimination and participated in educational efforts to eliminate anti-Semitism. Prominent ministers joined rabbis and community leaders to prevent rabid anti-Semites like Gerald L. K. Smith, leader of the America First Party, from using city-owned halls to preach his message of hate. Public educational endeavors were intensified by the Catholic archdiocese, the American Lutheran church, and other Christian groups. Congregations instituted pulpit exchanges between rabbis and priests. Candidates for public office were closely questioned about their attitudes toward civil rights. The onslaught of these

Synagogue women also participated in interfaith activities in an effort to educate and foster goodwill. Catherine Piccolo Louis, Estyr Peake, and Mrs. Max Granzberg admired a display with an international theme at the interfaith tea at Temple of Aaron, February 5, 1964.

activities, coupled with the economic boom that followed World War II, abated many overt manifestations of anti-Semitism and discrimination.[82]

Nevertheless Jews remained vigilant. The Minnesota Jewish Council, which evolved into the Minnesota Jewish Community Relations Council (JCRC) and then merged with the Anti-Defamation League of B'nai B'rith in 1975, continued to function as an educational and lobbying body on human rights and human relations. One legacy of the earlier troubles was a continuing commitment to civil rights and the fostering of a society of opportunity for all free from discrimination. As early supporters of the Urban League and the National Association for the Advancement of Colored People, Jewish leaders regarded civil rights for all as a guarantee of human rights for Jews.[83]

These attitudes help to explain the consistently liberal voting record of Minnesota Jews since the 1930s. Before that time, their allegiance had been almost evenly divided between Republican and opposition candidates, but after the advent of the New Deal, they voted overwhelmingly for Farmer-Labor and Democratic candidates. In the 1970s, however, as some successful Jews began voting their economic and social self-interest, the balance again shifted toward a more even Democratic-Farmer-Labor and Republican split.[84]

As they became more secure after the 1950s, Jews also ran for public office with greater frequency instead of occupying less visible staff and support positions as they had in the past. Their success at the polls, not only in legislative and local offices but also in the statewide arena, was one measure of declining prejudice. Arthur E. Naftalin served as mayor of Minneapolis from 1961 to 1969; Lawrence D. Cohen filled that post in St. Paul from 1972 to 1976 and Norman Coleman from 1994 to 2002. Rudolph (Rudy) E. Boschwitz was elected a United States Senator from Minnesota in 1978. Ironically, he was defeated in 1990 by Paul Wellstone, another Jew.[85]

For Alderman at Large
Vote For

| BENJAMIN MILAVETZ | X |

Election, Feb. 8, 1910

Jews have run for public office in many areas of the state. Benjamin Milavetz printed campaign cards in his ultimately unsuccessful effort to win a seat on the city council in 1910 in Virginia.

Jewish Communities until 1980

By the 1950s the early social and ethnic divisions between German and eastern European Jews in Minnesota had weakened. Communal integration had at last been achieved in part because the eastern Europeans and their descendants had attained geographic and occupational mobility and in part because of their numerical predominance in the Twin Cities. The bastions of German-Jewish exclusiveness slowly gave way until by the 1950s even in such old, elite institutions as Mount Zion Temple distinctions between the two groups had, for the most part, disappeared.[86]

The change had come gradually. Until the end of World War II, poverty among eastern European Jews was endemic. Most petty traders remained at that level for their entire lives, living a hand-to-mouth existence. Fewer than 1 in 10 were able to make the trek from peddling to small retail shops to the wholesale trade to real estate development that marked the successful. As late as 1936, some 126 Jewish families were displaced in the slum clearance that preceded the construction of the low-income Sumner Field Housing Project on the North Side of Minneapolis. Moreover Jews were eligible to occupy almost one-fourth of the living units in the completed project.[87]

For those Jews stuck at the lowest rung of the occupational and income ladder, hope centered on their children. A strong faith in formal education as the path to success led many parents to live on the edge of subsistence in order to ensure that one or more of their children would benefit from secondary school or college. Yet the full flowering of this upward effort was not apparent until after the 1940s. In 1949 a study by the Minneapolis Mayor's Council on Human Relations showed that 44% of the Jews were employed in clerical and sales jobs, while only 1.5% were professional or semiprofessional workers. Even more noteworthy was the finding that about 42% of Minneapolis Jews were craftsmen, factory employees, and laborers, but only a little over 6% occupied proprietary or managerial posts.

At that time about 60% of Minneapolis Jews still lived on the North Side, although the migration westward had already begun. After 1945 Jewish families in both the North and formerly stable South Sides moved first to such suburbs as St. Louis Park and Golden Valley and later farther west to Hopkins. Within the city itself, the areas of Kenwood, Lake of the Isles, and Lakes Harriet and Calhoun saw an expansion of Jewish settlement patterns. Not until the late 1960s, when the local consequences of the Black

Abe's Delicatessen was on Plymouth Avenue in Minneapolis along with a host of other businesses that catered to the North Side's Jewish population. Samuel S. Schwartz and his wife, Fay, ran the deli and posed with their children, May 17, 1948.

The Mount Sinai Hospital Auxiliary prepared in 1961 for their annual book fair; during one year the group used the entire courtyard of Southdale shopping mall.

revolution made themselves felt on the North Side, did the final remnants of Jewish population and institutions leave that part of the city.[88]

The postwar era saw a flowering of voluntary organizations. Men joined B'nai B'rith, synagogue men's clubs, and Jewish War Veterans; children took part in the B'nai B'rith Youth Organizations and synagogue youth groups. Women had an amazingly high membership rate; a 1958 Minneapolis communal study found that 85% of Jewish women belonged to organizations. Synagogue auxiliaries, the Mount Sinai Hospital Women's Auxiliary and Hadassah raised significant amounts of money for their causes while the St. Paul Section of NCJW's 1964 McKinley School project served as a model for the Headstart program, and a

Minneapolis section project provided hundreds of children in public schools with reading tutors.[89]

Dramatic changes occurred in the occupational distribution of Minneapolis Jewish men and women during the 25 years from 1945 to 1970. The influence of the school, the settlement house, and the cultural trait that emphasized education coupled with the G.I. Bill had assured that a significant number of the immigrants' children would be able to rise occupationally and economically. Although a small percentage had opted for sports or for petty crime and bootlegging after the onset of Prohibition in 1919, success was achieved largely through professional and mercantile pursuits. By 1971 less than 10% of all Jews in Minneapolis were craftsmen, factory operatives, laborers, and service workers; 90% were in professional, clerical, managerial, and proprietary occupations. Professional and technical employment accounted for 28.2% of the total; 41.4% of the men, 12.2% of the women, and 32.3% of all gainfully employed Minneapolis Jews were managers, proprietors, or administrators. Clerical and sales occupations engaged 21% of the males, 53% of the females, and almost 31% of all Minneapolis employed Jewish adults. In contrast was the

Brochin's Book and Gift Shop, which was located in St. Louis Park in 2000, sells Jewish ritual objects and clothing. Owner Barry Greenberg, wearing a tallit or a prayer shawl, posed in front of a display case in 1998.

Fannie Overman Goldfine, a successful Duluth business-woman, presided over the groundbreaking for Goldfine's discount store in 1961. Starting in 1922, she was in businesses with her husband, Abe, selling livestock, farm supplies, and furniture.

sharp decline in blue-collar occupations from 48.4% in 1947 to only 8.8% in 1971.[90]

The same study showed that the median household income for Minneapolis Jews was $1,805 higher than that reported for all Hennepin County households and that the educational level was substantially higher than that of their non-Jewish neighbors. Only 10% reported less than a high school education, and 63.4% cited college attendance, graduation, or postgraduate degrees. Nevertheless 17.8% of Minneapolis Jewish households in 1971 had annual incomes of less than $8,000.

Although no comparable statistics have been compiled for other Minnesota cities, it is probable that the findings would be similar for St. Paul. In Duluth, however, educational achievement and upward mobility have led to

Jewish out-migration. Informed opinion suggests that professional and educational achievement resulted in geographical migration to major metropolitan centers from the smaller market towns. The Jews remaining behind were mainly engaged in mercantile activities.[91]

Congregational or religious affiliation remained the single most significant mode of Jewish self-identification in Minnesota. Although comparable figures are not available for the rest of the state, a 1971–72 report on Minneapolis indicated that over 88% of all Jewish adults identified themselves with one of the three major branches of Judaism—52.9% with Conservatism, 27.5% with Reform, and 7.9% with Orthodoxy. (Of the remaining 12%, 2.9% were secular, 2.2% fell into the "other" category, and 6.7% did not reply.) Yet only 77% of the heads of households claimed congregational membership, and the records of synagogues affirmed that 65.7% were indeed members. Most knowledgeable observers believed that similar proportions existed in St. Paul and perhaps Duluth.[92]

In the same survey, a sample of approximately 10% of the community showed that nearly 90% of Minneapolis Jews over the age of six had completed at least one year of formal Jewish education. But its attractions were declining. In 1971–72 only 43% of the children aged 5 to 17 were enrolled in Jewish educational programs. In 1957 the same age group had a 55% attendance rate. Although most parents reported that they were highly satisfied with their children's learning experiences, the children themselves were not so enthusiastic.

Minnesota Jews were primarily an English-speaking people. In 1970, 9,209 had declared Yiddish as their mother tongue, but fewer and fewer were able to function in that language with each passing year. The cultural revival associated with the establishment of Israel had brought about increased efforts to teach the Hebrew language to the young, but few Minnesotans had more than a bare acquaintance with it. They might have been able to read Hebrew prayers, but most could not read, write, or speak the language.[93]

Immigration, Identity, and Continuity

According to the 1990 National Jewish Population Survey, trends such as movement to suburbs, increases in intermarriage, and decreases in synagogue membership and Jewish-directed philanthropy were continuing at the end of the 20th century. The 1993 St. Paul and 1994 Minneapolis Jewish population studies corroborated most of these trends. Within the Jewish community the findings were a source of disquiet as well as a call to action.[94]

During this same period the community was enriched by the arrival of a sizable number of Jews from the former Soviet Union. Disgusted with anti-Semitism that was used as a government tool and that inflamed Russia's centuries-long antipathy to Jews, they opted to emigrate. The first groups settled in Israel. They were followed by less ideological Jews who simply desired to live in a place where their children would enjoy equality of opportunity and who chose the United States. Usually referred to as Russian Jews or New Americans, they began arriving in Minnesota in 1972. By 2001 somewhere between 4,000 and 8,000 Jews settled in the state.[95]

The émigrés, often called "the Third Wave," were given refugee status by the federal government, allowing them housing benefits and access to health care. The Jewish community, which had long supported political efforts to allow Soviet Jews freedom to emigrate, rallied to support their long-lost brethren. Refugees were met at the airport by representatives of the Jewish Family Services (JFS) with whom they continued to meet at monthly intervals. They were escorted to apartments furnished by the Jewish community, which also provided them with rent stipends, one year of free tuition at Jewish day schools and Talmud Torahs, and free membership in synagogues and Jewish community centers. They enrolled in English classes at Jewish community centers as well. An American "anchor family" program provided a less institutional means of aiding the newcomers and introducing them to Jewish-American customs and rituals.

As with previous immigration waves, there were misunderstandings and misapprehensions on both sides. Minnesota's Jews perhaps naively expected to greet people similar to those portrayed in the musical *Fiddler on the Roof*. They were not ready for the tense engineers, factory managers, and professionals who alighted from the airplanes, speaking only Russian. The Russian Jews' lack of familiarity with Jewish holidays or synagogue rituals and, indeed, with the structure of an open society where Judaism was expressed by voluntary membership in organizations, synagogues, and philanthropic groups, was simply unbelievable.

And how could the Russian Jews live up to American expectations? After a half century of Bolshevism, the Russian Jews' concepts of Judaism and Jewish practices were quite different from those they now encountered. Their articulation of Judaism was that it was something "in their blood." It corresponded with the Soviet attribution of Judaism as one based on nationality or ethnicity. An encounter eerily reminiscent of that between German Jews and east European Jews and later between DPs and Jewish social service agencies took place. To be remade as Jews was humiliating; to find oneself dependent on agencies doubly so, particularly when so many of the refugees arrived with excellent educational credentials.

The Jewish Vocational Services (JVS), which refugees used when they needed help finding a job, became a locus of friction. Russian Jews arrived with a well-honed mistrust of government agencies, which they transferred to

JVS, feeling that the agency wanted to place them in the first available job rather than ones for which they had been educated. They could not believe that qualifications rather than connections were necessary to secure employment and were unwilling to admit that they might not be able to find suitable jobs until their English skills improved. Licensing requirements of professionals, such as doctors and dentists, proved almost insurmountable.

Despite misconceptions on both sides, the resettlement moved forward, aided by remarkable volunteers such as Felicia Weingarten. Having experienced the difficulties of immigrant status herself in the 1950s, she made it her business to visit every immigrant family in St. Paul, where, because of her fluency in one Slavic language—Polish—she was able to converse with and encourage them.

The Soviet Union halted emigration in 1981, which had several beneficial effects. Those already here found jobs and integrated themselves into the Jewish community to some degree. They wrote to relatives about the problems they would encounter if and when immigration resumed. When immigration recommenced in 1987, the Jewish Family Services were able to hire Russian-speaking case workers. The second consequence was that the original families were in a position to sponsor their relatives, who, therefore, did not qualify for refugee status.

According to JFS estimates, the Russian Jews accounted for approximately 10% of Minnesota's Jewish population in 2000. Despite the trauma of resettlement, within five years the employable members of the community generally found jobs commensurate with their training. The fact that there were enclaves in Eagan, Plymouth, Eden Prairie, and Maple Grove attests to their economic success. They had taken to capitalism as well, starting businesses such as stores that provided ethnic foods, a Russian-language newspaper, and a school where children learned the Russian language and other aspects of Russian culture.

Russian-Jewish immigrant Raisa Neydelman received a hug from her daughter Luba Neydelman as she celebrated becoming an American citizen in Minneapolis in September 1998.

Although their integration into the Twin Cities Jewish community had not been formally measured since 1981, St. Paul JFS caseworkers estimated that roughly 20%, mainly children and older people, were comfortable interacting with American Jews. The elderly, who had experienced some Jewish religious life in Russia, have used the resources provided by agencies such as the Jewish community centers. Some enjoyed attending synagogue services, and almost all found they could manage quite well on limited budgets. In fact, they joked that in America of all places they had found a socialist system that worked! Russian families, who thought public schools lacking in rigor, enrolled their children in Jewish day schools. Here Russian students could make friends and often led the class in subjects such as mathematics.

Marriage choices and levels of Jewish observance were also indicators of integration. JFS workers estimated that about 50% marry other Russians. They appeared to be celebrating Jewish holidays. Jewish rites such as *brit milah* (circumcision), bar and bat mitzvah, weddings, and funerals seem to be well observed and now have their own Russian flavor. The Lubavitchers, who have long supported outreach to Soviet Jews, helped found a Russian-speaking synagogue in St. Paul in the 1990s. Several Russian Jews have served on Jewish agency boards, but even though some have made close friendships, particularly with anchor families, there still was no great acceptance from the long-established Jewish community. Members of the third wave were resigned to the double lens that immigrant status imparts but were relieved, knowing that their children would grow up feeling comfortable in America and in the American Jewish community.[96]

During the same period the community responded to the influx of Russian Jews, it was also responding to new challenges. In effect it was two sides of the same coin: How to incorporate Russian-born Jews and how to retain American-born Jews, inculcating both with a sense of allegiance to Jewish communal institutions.

The Jewish population increased in the late 20th century, chiefly due to immigration. A 1993 St. Paul United Jewish Fund and Council (UJFC) study counted 11,100 Jews. A similar study conducted in Minneapolis in 1994 found 31,560 Jews, and Jewish households made up 3.5 % of all households in Hennepin County, up from the 21,638 individuals enumerated in the 1971 Minneapolis Jewish population study.[97]

Since 1980 Jews have continued to flock to suburbia. After St. Paul itself, those suburbs most popular were the Mendota Heights area, followed by the north and south suburbs. Minneapolis was attractive to single Jews, while married couples and families chose to live in suburbs like St. Louis Park, Golden Valley, Hopkins, Edina, and Plymouth. New synagogues, such as Beth Jacob in St. Paul and Beth Shalom in Minneapolis, have built in the suburbs to serve the population living there, while Adath Jeshurun relocated to Minnetonka for the same reason.[98]

The trends toward higher education, professional careers, and higher than average earnings intensified. In Minneapolis, for example, of those under the age of 35, 86% had undergraduate college degrees or had done postgraduate work. The Minneapolis survey reported the occupational breakdown: professional—male 43% and female 34%; executive/managerial—male 9% and female 7%; sales—male 10% and female 6%; technician/support—male 4% and female 4%; service—male 4% and female 4%; other—male 9% and female 6%. The figures hardly differed for St. Paul where over 50% of women were in the work force full time with almost another 25% working part time. The median income in Minneapolis was higher than the county median by almost $5,000.[99]

Commitments to Jewish institutions and voluntary organizations were diminishing. The St. Paul survey counted only 43% who were members of a Jewish organization other than a synagogue. Synagogue membership also continued to decrease. In Minneapolis it stood at 49%, of which 54% were Conservative, 39% Reform, and 4% Orthodox.[100]

Most telling in the 1994 Minneapolis Jewish Federation study was a section titled "the religion of Jewish household members." The Federation defined the Jewish household as one "where at least one head of the household was born Jewish, was raised Jewish, has a parent who is Jewish, or considers himself or herself to be Jewish." Under this definition, there were an estimated 38,570 Jewish households containing an estimated 7,010 non-Jews. This redefinition of Jewish identity came about because of the sharp increase in intermarriage. In Minneapolis, for example, 66% of marriages since 1990 were mixed.[101]

The concern, of course, was with continuity, and the locus of anxiety was the Jewish identity of intermarried couples' children. The studies showed that in the Twin Cities somewhere between 25 and 33% of children under 18 in households with a non-Jewish parent were being raised

The Birthright Israel program funds 10-day trips for young adults, ages 18–26, who have never been to Israel on a peer educational tour. The goal is to reinforce Jewish identity and strengthen ties to Israel. These students from Hillel paused on a hill overlooking Jerusalem on a study trip in 1998.

as Jewish while an equal percentage were raised as Christians. Put another way, in St. Paul, only 17% of children in households with mixed-faith parents received any Jewish education.[102]

Alongside the demographic reports there were other studies indicating that Jewish life might lose the next generation if it continued to concentrate solely on Holocaust remembrance and support of Israel, important though those concerns were. There was evidence as well that younger American Jews, like members of other white ethnic groups, viewed their Jewish identity as a choice rather than a fixed entity. Among Jewish academicians, the pessimists argued that a focus on ethnic food, Holocaust museums, and Jewish book fairs would create a Judaism hollowed of content, while optimists retorted that Jewish life would continue to be transformed in the encounter with America.[103]

Jewish reactions to the 1990 national and the 1993 and 1994 local studies continue to evolve. Clearly without continued immigration, it appeared that the next generation of Jews would be smaller and less committed to continued support of a Jewish community and Jewish interests abroad. Perhaps the most robust response was that of the Minneapolis Jewish Federation, which in 1994 began planning a Commission on Jewish Identity and Continuity in order to provide "new ways for people to connect to the Jewish community." Once organized, the commission created several task forces to reach out and involve unaffiliated and interfaith families, Jewish singles, and teens. It rethought delivery of Jewish education from birth to grave and even established a committee to integrate the arts into Jewish ritual practices.[104]

Synagogues were affected by the study as well. One way they reacted was by working with the Identity and Continuity Task Force to welcome intermarried couples and their children. Still another was by offering members various ways to connect to core Judaism. Several Conservative synagogues responded by, for example, urging members to assume the observance of kashrut (Jewish dietary laws) or celebrate Shabbat (Sabbath) in a way that sanctified the day. Adults were encouraged to study Torah and learn the Torah cantillations. The synagogues had already become more egalitarian, and female rabbis, cantors, and synagogue presidents were not uncommon.[105]

By contrast, the Orthodox community appears to have become stronger. Several Orthodox synagogues in St. Louis Park constructed an *eruv*—a boundary line enclosing an area within which observant Jews were permitted to carry objects on the Sabbath. The Lubavitch movement developed as well. The Minnesota community was founded when the Lubavitch Rebbe (holy man) sent several of his followers to St. Paul to encourage Jews to return to traditional religious practices. Beginning with a small group in

An intergenerational group concentrated on their studies at the Torah Academy in Minneapolis in 1981.

the 1960s, the community numbered about 200 families and maintained several synagogues and educational institutions in the Twin Cities in 2001. Their publications reached thousands of Jews in the state, and they also had a presence in the Rochester and Duluth communities.[106]

There has been, as well, a desire for more ways to express Judaism through meaningful social action. Religious leaders invoked an ancient concept called *Tikkun Olam* (repair of the world), one that dovetailed nicely with service initiatives of Christian and American civic groups. One such group was Jewish Community Action (JCA), which was founded in 1995 to pursue goals of racial, social, and economic justice and to reach out to interested but unaffiliated Jews interested in grass-roots organizing. JCA built partnerships with communities of color and other faith-based groups to work for affordable housing, fairer immigration laws, an end to racial profiling, and reinvestment in poorer communities. With anti-Semitism on the

Toni Collins (second from right), manager of the South Central Branch of City-County Federal Credit Union, accepted an investment check from Jewish Community Action board chair Marcy Shapiro along with staff Frank Hornstein and Vic Rosenthal in 2001. They planned to use the funds to help with inner-city redevelopment.

decrease, the JCRC also instituted programs that, for example, supplied volunteers to communities hit with natural disasters and fostered cooperation with other faith-based groups to alleviate poverty.[107]

Another response to the need for more Jewish content has been the growth of Jewish day schools and the support for Jewish camping experiences. Both St. Paul and Minneapolis established nondenominational schools in the 1980s and added a Twin Cities middle school in the 1990s, which together serve about 500 students. Torah Academy, established in the 1940s, continued to serve the Orthodox community. Scholarships were more readily available through synagogues and the Federations for a variety of Jewish campers and for visits to Israel.

Conclusion

At the beginning of a new century, the Twin Cities Jewish community focused on the future. With anti-Semitism low and acceptance high, most Minnesota Jews felt quite secure. The elderly were provided with a range of living options from assisted living to nursing home care on a Minneapolis suburban campus. In 2001 both the St. Paul and Minneapolis Federations instituted capital campaigns to repair structures built in the 1950s, to reconfigure existing community spaces, and to build new structures. Federations and synagogues, once suspicious of each other, were cooperating on programming and planning to share spaces. The Federations and synagogues also began conceptualizing how services might be delivered in the 21st century and, indeed, what services would be needed. Disseminating information and education via the internet was already common and no doubt would increase.

As another sign of the Jewish community's maturity and its deep roots in Minnesota, several history-conscious people founded the Jewish Historical Society in 1984 and in 2001 placed its archives in the Elmer L. Andersen Library at the University of Minnesota, further enriching Jewish studies on that campus. Support for Israel continued to be high, and student programs in Israel grew in popularity. While harmony did not reign supreme, Minnesota's Jews felt confident they could meet the challenges of the new century and create a multifaceted Judaism that would enrich their lives and that of their children and enhance the democratic ideals that they and all Americans endorsed.

Personal Account:
An Immigrant's Story

by Charles Upin

Charles Upin was born in 1891 in Sade, Lithuania, then a part of Russia. His father was a butcher who shipped meat to larger cities such as Riga. He emigrated in 1912 to Norfolk, Virginia, where he had an uncle. Shortly thereafter he left to join another uncle in Chippewa Falls, Wisconsin. He joined the navy in 1917, where the worst enemy turned out to be influenza. Returning to Chippewa Falls, he remained until 1921, when he opened a store in Albert Lea. He lived there for the next 50 years, raising a family and participating in numerous organizations such as Rotary, Masons, American Legion, Chamber of Commerce, and the school board. His story, while in many respects a typical immigrant entrepreneur account, illuminates an aspect of American Jewish life that has not been fully told—that of creating and maintaining a Jewish life in a small town. The following is compressed from an oral history done with Upin in 1982, two years before his death, by Marilyn Chiat, who, at the time, was director of the Project to Document Jewish Settlers in Minnesota. Schloff edited the account, combining sentences, rearranging text, and omitting breaks in order to make it more readable. Upin's oral history is at JHSUM.

The reason I came to this country was that I was supposed to report to the Russian army. I was twenty-one, you see, and not wishing to serve, I stole over the border. My father supplied me with hard bread and dry herring so I had something kosher to eat. I landed in Castle Garden, and I had a train ticket to Norfolk, where I joined an uncle. There I delivered meat for his kosher butcher shop. He used to give me the orders to deliver in a basket. Well, I asked for directions, but I couldn't speak English, and people didn't understand my Russian. So by the time I got to people's homes it was way after noon, and they began to complain. I held that job for about ten days, and I could see that he wasn't satisfied. And I thought, before I get fired I'm going to quit.

So I wrote a letter to another uncle I had in Chippewa Falls, Wisconsin. He sent me a train ticket, and when I got there, they found me a job

Jews who lived in small towns frequently ran dry-goods stores. Charles Upin's store in Albert Lea carried a full line of men's clothing in 1925.

in a sugar beet factory. I worked there in the fall of the year, and then they closed for the season. So they thought it would be nice if they bought me a horse and buggy and sent me around peddling. Well, I wasn't overly enthused about doing that. I finally got a job in a furniture factory, but I was injured on a saw blade, so I got laid off. Finally, I got a job with my uncle's son who had a clothing store—washing windows, keeping stock, sweeping the floor, and all that. In the meantime he said, "You're going to learn a trade." In a few years I was the store manager. In 1917 this son joined the navy. I thought, if it was good for him to join the navy it would be good for me too. After World War I, I returned to Chippewa Falls. I went to night school. It helped me a lot, especially with pronunciation. I'm the type of person that if I don't know something, I'll repeat or rewrite a word ten times until I perfect it.

During the war I used to send my family money, but I didn't know whether or not they got it. After the war I got a letter telling me that my father had died. And I had my mother and seven brothers and sisters there. I brought over the whole family. Then I found that there wasn't enough money to go around, so I thought I'd better try to go into business for myself.

I didn't have any capital and had no credit. So a brother of mine who lived in St. Paul got me together with a man named Simon Lasker that he knew. We went around searching for locations, and Albert Lea seemed to be a town that I would like. I always lived in small towns. I never lived in a big city, with the exception of ten days in Norfolk.

We started in business in September 1921. We started with all sorts of clothing, but little by little we concentrated on men's clothing. We called it the St. Paul Clothing House at that time. The bank was willing to loan us money because my partner had a good reputation and already had a store in Fairmont.

At that time there weren't too many Jewish people living in Albert Lea. There was a German Jew by the name of Strauss, who had a clothing store. A family by the name of Hirsch had a hide and fur business, and there were the Gendlers in scrap metal.

This Mr. Strauss was also a vice president of the bank that we borrowed money from. Every time we made a payment, he used to give us our promissory note back. He used to sort of glance at the inventory, and I could tell he was counting the stock to see how much we had sold. He was a short man with quite a stomach and a heavy white moustache. And he would look up, and I knew he was counting the shirt boxes. And many of them were empty, but he didn't know that. In 1947 I bought out my partner. At that time we had three stores—Albert Lea, Faribault, and Grand Rapids.

I met and married my wife in 1924. Her parents had a little general store in Aberdeen, and her mother passed away in 1922. So she came to live with her sister and brother-in-law who owned a ladies ready-to-wear in Albert Lea. We were married at a Jewish club in St. Paul. We had two sons.

When we were first married we (Austin and Albert Lea Jews) rented a hall for Rosh Hashanah and Yom Kippur, and we used to have a man come out from St. Paul to lead services. People came in from smaller communities as well.

I belong to the Temple of Aaron (in St. Paul). In fact I was on the board of directors. I used to take a train in those days and stay overnight for the meetings. My boys were bar mitzvahed there. I used to have a man from St. Paul come here to teach them. He would arrive early Sunday and teach them, then go back on the last train of the day. After they were bar mitzvahed, the boys and I would put on our *tallis* (prayer shawl) and *tfillim* (phylacteries) and say prayers every morning.

We kept kosher, but it wasn't 100 percent kosher. In those days getting meat here was very, very hard. But whenever we went to the Cities we always brought back kosher meat. We used to invite our non-Jewish friends over for Friday night, and my wife always lit the candles, and we used to say Kiddush.

I first joined B'nai B'rith in 1917, and we met in Eau Claire. We started a B'nai B'rith lodge for Austin and Albert Lea in 1939, and I was the first president.

I always said, "Whenever I build a home I'm going to have a place where we can be together with Jewish people." In 1955 I built a new home. On the lower level I had a room that we used for our Jewish services, Seders, and B'nai B'rith meetings. We would have it one month in my house and one month at Usem's Garage in Austin.

Years ago, before the United Jewish Appeal when no one came out here to solicit I just appointed myself to be chairman. And we used to collect money and send it away. I would keep five percent for the *mishulachim* (Yiddish for traveling solicitors for religious Jewish causes). They used to come by train and head for a dentist right across the street from us by the name of Kaplan. He wasn't Jewish. He used to tell them, "Go over to St. Paul Clothing House and ask for Charlie Upin." I never turned anyone down. Never.

I was chairman of the Board of Education for twelve years. I never campaigned. My neighbor went out and got up a petition to file my name. I always voted Democratic, but Albert Lea is a very strong Republican town. After one bad experience where I lost a customer, I never publicly went out and expressed my opinion again. I felt, I'm here to make a living. If I lose this store, nobody is going to put me back in business.

We socialized plenty with non-Jews as well. They used to come over to our house for dinner, and we were invited to theirs. They were our friends, and I contributed to their churches as well. I attended their churches for weddings and funerals.

I like Albert Lea very much. In my will I left money for the city and the high school libraries. I specified that they purchase books of Jewish history and culture because I wanted the people to know about these things.

Jewish people like me who settled here—we couldn't afford to go to school. We had our families and made our living here. But our children, when they grew up, began to fulfill our wishes to have a son who was a lawyer or a doctor or something like that. And they didn't come back. Jewish young people don't live in these small communities anymore.

For Further Reading

Chiat, Marilyn J., and Chester Proshan. *We Rolled Up Our Sleeves: A History of the United Jewish Fund and Council and Its Beneficiary Agencies.* St. Paul: United Jewish Fund and Council of St. Paul, 1985.

Gordon, Albert I. *Jews in Transition.* Minneapolis: University of Minnesota Press, 1949.

Hoffman, William. *Those Were the Days.* Minneapolis: T. S. Denison, 1957.

Holmquist, June D., ed., *They Chose Minnesota: A Survey of the State's Ethnic Groups* (St. Paul: Minnesota Historical Society Press, 1981).

Minda, Albert G. *The Story of Temple Israel, Minneapolis, Minnesota: A Personal Account.* Minneapolis, 1971.

Plaut, W. Gunther. *The Jews in Minnesota: The First Seventy-five Years.* American Jewish Communal Histories, no. 3. New York: American Jewish Historical Society, 1959.

———. *Mount Zion, 1856–1956: The First Hundred Years.* St. Paul: North Central Pub. Co., 1956.

Schloff, Linda Mack. *"And Prairie Dogs Weren't Kosher": Jewish Women in the Upper Midwest Since 1855.* St. Paul: Minnesota Historical Society Press, 1996.

Notes

1. W. Gunther Plaut, *The Jews in Minnesota: The First Seventy-five Years*, 8–15, 123–25 (New York, 1959); John Syrjamaki, "Mesabi Communities: A Study of Their Development," 128, 131, Ph.D. thesis, Yale University, 1940; Linda Mack Schloff, "Overcoming Geography: Jewish Religious Life in Four Market Towns," in *Minnesota History*, 1–14 (Spring 1988); Chester Proshan, "Eastern European Jewish Immigrants and Their Children on the Minnesota Iron Range, 1890s–1980s," Ph.D. thesis, University of Minnesota, 1998.

2. On the origins of Jewish mass migration to the U.S., see Zoza Szajkowski, "How the Mass Migration to America Began," in *Jewish Social Studies*, 4:291–310 (Oct. 1942); Ezekiel Lifschutz, "The First Russo-Jewish Mass Immigration and the American Jews" (Yiddish), in *Yivo Bleter*, 4:312 (Nov.–Dec. 1932); Gerald Sorin, *A Time for Building: The Third Migration, 1880–1920*, Vol. 3 of *The Jewish People In America* ((Baltimore 1992), Henry Feingold, ed.; Salo Baron, *The Russian Jew Under Tsars and Soviets* (New York, 1964).

3. On the religious-cultural traits of the eastern European immigants, see Hutchins Hapgood, *Spirit of the Ghetto: Studies of the Jewish Quarter of New York* (New York, 1976); Irving Howe, *World of Our Fathers* (New York, 1976); Moses Rischin, *The Promised City: New York's Jews, 1870–1914* (Cambridge, Mass., 1977).

4. H. S. Lenfeld, "The Jews of the United States, Numbers and Distribution," in *American Jewish Year Book, 5700*, 41:185 (Philadelphia, 1939), hereafter cited as *AJYB*; "Jewish Population in the United States, 1995," in *AJYB, 1996*. See also note 97, below.

A survey of the Minneapolis Jewish population in 1936 produced a count of 16,260, whereas the *AJYB, 5703*, 44:426 (1942), estimate for 1937 was 20,700. The survey method, however, may well have resulted in an undercount; see Sophia M. Robison, "The Jewish Population of Minneapolis, 1936," in Sophia M. Robison, ed., *Jewish Population Studies*, 152–59 (New York, 1943).

5. For a succinct summary of the vast literature on Jewish identity, see Salo W. Baron, *The Jewish Community*, 3–10 (Reprint; Westport, Conn., 1972); for a discussion focusing on St. Paul, see Arnold Dashefsky and Howard Shapiro, *Ethnic Identification Among American Jews*, 1–31 (Lexington, Mass., 1974).

6. Albert I. Gordon, *Jews in Transition*, 12–14 (Minneapolis, 1949); Plaut, *Jews in Minnesota*, 9–10, 39. For a firsthand account, see Amelia Ullmann, "Saint Paul Forty Years Ago," 1896, MHS, portions published in *Minnesota History* as "Spring Comes to the Frontier," 33 (Spring 1953): 194–200, "Frontier Business Trip, 34 (Spring 1954): 17–27, and "Pioneer Homemaker," 34 (Autumn 1954): 96–105.

7. W. Gunther Plaut, *Mount Zion, 1856–1956: The First Hundred Years*, 11–14 (St. Paul, [1956]) and *Jews in Minnesota*, 33–35.

8. Plaut, *Jews in Minnesota*, 16–21 (on Noah), 35, 46, 58 (on Cardozo).

9. Plaut, *Jews in Minnesota*, 47, 54–57, 312; Hiram D. Frankel, "The Jews of St. Paul," in *Reform Advocate* (Chicago), Nov.

16, 1907, p. 45; Sons of Jacob, *75th Anniversary Book* (St. Paul, 1953).

10. *American Israelite* (Cincinnati), Dec. 24, 1875; Ruby Danenbaum, "A History of the Jews of Minneapolis," in *Reform Advocate*, Nov. 16, 1907, pp. 7, 13, 20, 29; Albert G. Minda, *The Story of Temple Israel, Minneapolis, Minnesota: A Personal Account*, 4 (Minneapolis, 1971).

11. Plaut, *Jews in Minnesota*, 57, 95; Minda, *Story of Temple Israel*, 4–7.

12. Here and below, see Plaut, *Jews in Minnesota*, 51, 58–60; Danenbaum and Frankel, in *Reform Advocate*, Nov. 16, 1907, pp. 8, 30, 47. On civic involvement, the *St. Paul Globe* reported on Feb. 3, 1897, that "During the last year . . . the Hebrews of the city contributed half of the money given to charity in St. Paul"; quoted in Linda Mack Schloff, *"And Prairie Dogs Weren't Kosher": Jewish Women in the Upper Midwest Since 1855*, 160 (St. Paul, 1996).

13. On B'nai B'rith, see Debra Dash Moore, *B'nai B'rith and the Challenge of Ethnic Leadership* (Albany, 1981). For more on the B'nai B'rith lodges in Minnesota, see Hiram D. Frankel Papers and Independent Order of B'nai B'rith, Chicago, Papers (Grand Lodge District Number 6), both MHS.

14. On marriage outside the group, see Gordon, *Jews in Transition*, 206; Plaut, *Mount Zion*, 23.

15. Here and two paragraphs below, see *St. Paul Pioneer Press*, July 16, 17, 18, 20, 23, 26, 1882; Plaut, *Jews in Minnesota*, 90–95. For more on conditions leading to the mass emigration, see Simon Dubnow, *History of the Jews in Russia and Poland*, 2:269–330 (Reprint, Philadelphia, 1946); Baron, *The Russian Jew*, 76–118.

16. Mark Wischnitzer, *To Dwell in Safety: The Story of Jewish Migration Since 1800* (Philadelphia, 1948), 39, 44–49. The *St. Paul Pioneer Press*, July 17, 1882, attributed the shipment of the 200 refugee Jews to the Mansion House Committee, which it erroneously located in Liverpool, England.

17. The announced policy of the Russian government was to induce mass migration, force conversion, or use extermination to eliminate Jews from the empire. This policy, formulated by Constantine Pobiedonostsev, the Procurator of the Holy Synod, was effected by expelling Jews from Moscow (1891), inciting pogroms by the Black Hundreds, and stimulating peasant attacks on Jewish communities, in addition to passing legal prohibitions against Jews in designated occupations. Mass Jewish emigration also resulted from the internal revolutionary upheaval and defeat by Japan in 1905. See Dubnow, *Jews in Russia*, 2:336–73, 399–413; Wischnitzer, *To Dwell in Safety*, 67–70, 105.

18. Wischnitzer, *To Dwell in Safety*, 66; Minnesota population estimated from *AJYB, 5688*, 29:242 (1927), and U.S. Census Bureau, *Special Reports, Religious Bodies: 1926*, 2:648.

19. Plaut, *Jews in Minnesota*, 95, 110–14. For fictional re-creations based on life in Minneapolis and St. Paul, see Myron Brinig, *Singermann* (New York, 1929); Jennie Rosenholtz, *Upon Thy Doorposts* (New York, 1936); Harry Bloom, *Sorrow Laughs* (New York, 1959); and a series by William Hoffman: *Those Were the Days* (Minneapolis, 1957), *Tales of Hoffman* (Minneapolis, 1961), *Mendel* (South Brunswick, N.J., 1969).

20. Plaut, *Jews in Minnesota*, 101.

21. Wischnitzer, *To Dwell in Safety*, 78–82. For more on the philanthropist, see

Samuel Joseph, *History of the Baron de Hirsch Fund* (New York, 1935).

22. Plaut, *Mount Zion*, 56–58, and *Jews in Minnesota*, 96. For an excellent recent account, see J. Sanford Rikoon, "Jewish Farm Settlements in America's Heartland," 105–33, in *Rachel Calof's Story: Jewish Homesteader on the Northern Plains*, J. Sanford Rikoon, ed. (Bloomington, 1995). See also Julius Goldman, *Report on the Colonization of the Russian Refugees in the West*, 1–3, 6, 15–24 (New York, 1882); Julius Goldman Papers in the Jewish division of the New York Public Library.

23. Leonard G. Robinson, "Agricultural Activities of the Jews in America," in *AJYB, 5673*, 14:61, 93 (1912); Plaut, *Jews in Minnesota*, 96–109; Cyrus Adler, *Jacob H. Schiff: His Life and Letters*, 2:87 (Garden City, N.Y., 1929). The Schiff-Hill correspondence is also in President's File, Great Northern Railway Papers, MHS.

24. Robinson, in *AJYB, 5673*, 14:77, 78 (1912).

25. Melinda Beth Weinblatt, "Minnesota Bound: A Perspective on the IRO and Immigrant Satisfaction," 122, Senior honors thesis, Brandeis University, 1994, copy in Jewish Historical Society of the Upper Midwest (JHSUM). See also Sorin, *A Time for Building*, 63–64.

26. Bernard Marinbach, *Galveston: Ellis Island of the West* (Albany, 1983); Wischnitzer, *To Dwell in Safety*, 127–30.

27. Frankel, in *Reform Advocate*, Nov. 16, 1907, pp. 45–47; *American Jewish World*, Sept. 22, 1922, p. 55; Plaut, *Jews in Minnesota*, 157–59, 189. Population figures, here and below, are rough estimates, generally composites of synagogue and society memberships. On the difficulties of gauging populations, see *AJYB, 5661*, 2:624 (1900).

28. Plaut, *Jews in Minnesota*, 110, 117.

29. Gordon, *Jews in Transition*, 14, 19; Minda, *Story of Temple Israel*, 6; Herbert S. Rutman, "Defense and Development: A History of Minneapolis Jewry, 1930–1950," 8–10, Ph.D. thesis, University of Minnesota, 1970.

30. Gordon, *Jews in Transition*, 6; Calvin F. Schmid, *Social Saga of Two Cities: An Ecological and Statistical Study*, 77–79, 151, 152 (Minneapolis, 1937); "North Side Memories: An Oral History of Minnesota's Largest Jewish Neighborhood," *Upper Midwest Jewish History*, 2 (Fall 2000); oral histories with former North Side residents, JHSUM.

31. Duluth's Orthodox synagogues were Tifereth Israel (1892 or 1893), founded by Russian Jews; Adas Israel (late 1890s), founded by Lithuanian Jews; and B'nai Israel (late 1890s). Temple Emanuel, founded in 1891, was a Reform congregation. Plaut, *Jews in Minnesota*, 123–25, 132–39; Thelma C. Covner, "The New Wilderness: Building the Jewish Community in Duluth, Minnesota, 1870–1975," 3–10, typescript, [1975?], copy in MHS; Jewish Welfare Federation of Duluth, *Social, Recreational, and Educational Survey of the Jewish Community of Duluth, 1944*, 5–20 ([Duluth, 1944]); Agudath Achim Synagogue, *31 Years of Jewish Life on Iron Range of Northern Minnesota*, 8–31 (Hibbing, 1938); Proshan, "Eastern European Jewish Immigrants," 290–336. For the date of 1869, Schloff is indebted to a research communication from Joanne Sher.

32. Schloff, "Overcoming Geography," 1–14. For information on Rochester's synagogue, see Eliot Baskin, "B'nai Israel Synagogue," 27, in *A Legacy of Pride: The American Jewish World*, 75 (October 31, 1986); e-mail communication from Rabbi David Freedman, July 16, 2001.

33. Nathan Goldberg, *Occupational Patterns of American Jewry*, 15–19 (New York, 1947); Judith R. Kramer and Seymour Leventman, *Children of the Gilded Ghetto*, 51 (New Haven, Conn., 1961). For an analysis of Twin Cities Jewish women's employment in 1910, see Schloff, *Prairie Dogs*, 115–54.

34. Plaut, *Jews in Minnesota*, 112, 129, 156; Gordon, *Jews in Transition*, 18; Hoffman, *Those Were the Days*, 135–39.

35. Morris Kaplan and Mildred Kaplan Light, "Reminiscences," unpublished manuscript in Morris Kaplan and Family Papers, MHS. For Salet, see Schloff, "Overcoming Geography," 3.

36. Council of Jewish Federations and Welfare Funds, *Minneapolis Jewish Communal Survey*, 3:1–3 ([Minneapolis, 1936]); Frankel, in *Reform Advocate*, Nov. 16, 1907, p. 41. On Jewish business families, see, for example, the Papers of Hiram D. Frankel, of Joseph H. Schanfeld, and of Fanny F. Brin, all MHS. Even for those who achieved modest success, economic gains were, at times, precarious. The depression of 1893 drove many Jewish merchants to the brink of failure, and cries for reductions in their synagogue obligations reached a peak in 1894–95. Most survived these difficulties, but their economic success should not be exaggerated; Minda, *Story of Temple Israel*, 6.

37. Plaut, *Jews in Minnesota*, 56, 115–21, 202; Gordon, *Jews in Transition*, 19–21, 71–73, 152–63; Danenbaum, in *Reform Advocate*, Nov. 16, 1907, pp. 34, 38. St. Paul's Orthodox congregations were: Sons of Jacob (1872), known as the Polish synagogue; Sons of Zion (1883), formed by immigrants from Russia; Beth Hamedrash Hagodol (1888); Russian Brotherhood (1888); Sharey Hesed va-Emet (ca. 1900);

and Sons of Abraham (1900). Sons of Moses and Adath Yeshurun were organized in the early 1900s. The latter three along with Sons of Jacob were located near the state capitol. Sons of Jacob and Sons of Abraham later relocated in the Hill District. Around 1954 Adath Yeshurun, Sons of Moses, and Sons of Abraham merged to form Gedaliah Leib, which met in the old Mount Zion building on Holly and Avon. The other synagogues mentioned served the vast immigrant population on the West Side Flats.

Minneapolis' South Side synagogues were: Adath Jeshurun (1884); Rumanian Hebrew (1888), the forerunner of B'nai Abraham (1896); Nachlus Israel (1896); and Agudas Achim (1902). On the North Side were: Ohel Jacob (1888); Beth Medrash Hagodol (1888); Anshei Russia (1890), which changed its name to Mikro Kodesh in 1895; Tiferes B'nai Israel (1890), which became Tiferes B'nai Jacob in 1920; Anshei Tavrig (1902), which merged with Gemilas Chesed in 1915; Beth Aaron (1905), later called Sharai Zedeck.

38. Henry L. Feingold, *Zion in America: The Jewish Experience from Colonial Times to the Present* (New York, 1974), 96, 112; David Philipson, *The Reform Movement in Judaism*, 334–39 (Rev. ed., New York, 1931). For more on the 19th-century organizer of Reform Judaism in the U.S., see Isaac Meyer Wise, *Reminiscences* (New York, 1901); J. G. Heller, *Isaac M. Wise, His Life Work and Thought* (New York, 1965); Plaut, *Mount Zion*, 35.

39. Plaut, *Mount Zion*, 74–76, and *Jews in Minnesota*, 183–90.

40. Rutman, "Defense and Development," 58–62; Plaut, *Jews in Minnesota*, 190; Michael G. Rapp, "Samuel N. Deinard and the Unification of Jews in Minne-

apolis," in *Minnesota History*, 43:213–21 (Summer 1973).

41. Here and below, see Feingold, *Zion in America*, 179–93. On the development of Conservative Judaism in the U.S., see Moshe Davis, *The Emergence of Conservative Judaism: The Historical School in 19th Century America* (Philadelphia, 1965); for the practices and beliefs, see Marshall Sklare, *Conservative Judaism: An American Religious Movement* (New York, 1972).

42. Here and below, see Plaut, *Jews in Minnesota*, 119, 195–207, 314; Gordon, *Jews in Transition*, 153, 157–59, 162. Ohel Jacob and Beth Medrash Hagodol merged to form Kenesseth Israel. On the other synagogues, see note 38, above.

43. Berman's observations of membership and programs at Mount Zion and Temple Israel, 1962–80, and discussion with Rabbi Max Shapiro, Temple Israel, December 1980. The Bar and Bat Mitzvahs are rituals in which boys and girls, upon turning 13, are accepted as adult members of the faith.

44. Covner, "New Wilderness," 10, 21.

45. Mount Zion's HLBS subsequently divided into a ladies' auxiliary and the Jewish Relief Society of St. Paul; see Plaut, *Jews in Minnesota*, 57, 141–43, 153, and *Mount Zion* (where the name was given as the Ladies Hebrew Benevolent Society); Danenbaum, in *Reform Advocate*, Nov. 16, 1907, p. 20; *American Israelite*, Oct. 15, 1903, p. 3. Minute books and annual reports of the HLBS (St. Paul) are in MHS. See also Schloff, *Prairie Dogs*, 159–62.

46. Marilyn J. Chiat and Chester Proshan, *We Rolled Up Our Sleeves: A History of the United Jewish Fund and Council and Its Beneficiary Agencies*, 49–56 (St. Paul, 1985). For an overview of women's involvement in Upper Midwest synagogues, see Schloff, *Prairie Dogs*, 155–89.

47. Gordon, *Jews in Transition*, 39; Plaut, *Jews in Minnesota*, 221–23; Rutman, "Defense and Development," 85–88. See also Annual Reports, 1930, 1931, and minutes of the Jewish Family Welfare Association, Jewish Family and Children's Service Papers, MHS; Chiat and Proshan, *We Rolled Up Our Sleeves*, 49–56.

48. Plaut, *Jews in Minnesota*, 218–24; Gordon, *Jews in Transition*, 40; *American Jewish World*, Jan. 31, 1930, p. 4, Nov. 16, 1945, p. 11. For more on family welfare, relief, and care for the aged, see Council of Jewish Federations and Welfare Funds, *Minneapolis Jewish Communal Survey*, 1:1–9 ([Minneapolis, 1936]).

49. Gordon, *Jews in Transition*, 10; Council of Jewish Federations, *Minneapolis Jewish Communal Survey*, 3:2; Rutman, "Defense and Development," 89–97; [Rhoda G. Lewin], *Minneapolis Federation for Jewish Service: Moving Into the 80's*, 3–6 ([Minneapolis, 1980]); *American Jewish World*, Feb. 7, 1930, p. 3. Duluth followed a similar pattern of consolidation, first of social service agencies and then of all Jewish communal organizations. See Ida B. Davis Papers, MHS.

50. Danenbaum, in *Reform Advocate*, Nov. 16, 1907, p. 30; Gordon, *Jews in Transition*, 173–75; Plaut, *Jews in Minnesota*, 120, 138; Rutman, "Defense and Development," 44–46.

51. Oral histories, loan association pamphlets, ephemera, JHSUM.

52. Plaut, *Jews in Minnesota*, 149–51, 230–36. *American Jewish World*, Sept. 22, 1922, p. 23, stated that the Minneapolis chapter was founded in 1893. See also Records of National Council of Jewish Women, JHSUM.

53. For more on Cohen, see Paula E. Hyman and Deborah Dash Moore, eds., *Jewish Women in America: An Historical Encyclopedia*, 1:248–49 (New York, 1997). See also Cohen's lesson plans in Minneapolis Section, National Council of Jewish Women, collection at JHSUM.

54. Plaut, *Jews in Minnesota*, 147–51. For Brin, see Barbara Stuhler, "Fanny Brin, Woman of Peace," in Barbara Stuhler and Gretchen Kreuler, eds., *Women of Minnesota: Selected Biographical Essays*, 284–300 (St. Paul, 1977, 1998); Ruth F. Brin, "She Heard Another Drummer: The Life of Fanny Brin and Its Implications for the Sociology of Religion," master's thesis, University of Minnesota, 1972. The Fanny Fligelman Brin Papers, MHS, contain comprehensive documentation of both the Twin Cities chapters and the national activities of the NCJW. For continuing class divisions of NCJW in Minneapolis, see Linda Mack Schloff, "Building Community, Building Bridges: Jewish American Women's Organizations in Minneapolis, 1945–1975," 128, Ph.D. thesis, University of Minnesota, 1998.

55. Here and below, see Plaut, *Jews in Minnesota*, 152–55; Hoffman, *Those Were the Days*, 163–69; Lorraine Esterly Pierce, "St. Paul's Lower West Side," 36–40, 65, 87, 89, 121, master's thesis, University of Minnesota, 1971; Neighborhood House Association Papers, MHS. The HLBS's minutes indicate that in 1895 it donated "one hundred dollars to the…woman's Council for the purpose of organizing an 'Industrial School.'" The "woman's Council" referred to was the local chapter of NCJW, which had recently been organized in the city by Rachel Haas, a Mount Zion congregant and HLBS member. The NCJW's membership was almost identical to that of the HLBS. For decades, NCJW meetings were held in the synagogue's vestry rooms.

56. Angelo Cohn, "A Long Way From Ninth Street," in *Identity* (Minneapolis), April 1971, p. 11; Plaut, *Jews in Minnesota*, 229; Gordon, *Jews in Transition*, 40, 182; *American Jewish World*, Feb. 7, 1919, p. 376, Mar. 7, 1919, p. 439. For a claim that the NCJW provided financial support for the Talmud Torah recreational and social service efforts, see Richard M. Chapman, "'To Do These Mitzvahs': Jewish Philanthropy and Social Service in Minneapolis, 1900–1950," 105, Ph.D. thesis, University of Minnesota, 1993.

Legacies of the St. Paul and Minneapolis settlement houses are two Jewish Community Centers, one in each city, which in 2001 continued to provide cultural and recreational opportunities to middle-class Jews. Each is in a predominantly Jewish neighborhood: St. Louis Park in Minneapolis and Highland Park in St. Paul. See, for example, Judith B. Erickson and Mitchel J. Lazarus, *The Jewish Community of Greater Minneapolis: A Population Study*, ch.13, p.1 (Minneapolis, 1972). For the St. Paul Jewish Community Center, see Chiat and Proshan, 33–37.

57. Here and below, see Plaut, *Jews in Minnesota*, 170–73; Erickson and Lazarus, *Jewish Community*, ch. 13, p. 10; *American Jewish World*, Sept. 22, 1922, pp. 18–20, 75, Oct. 26, 1951, p. 3. For an assessment of the role of Gordon, see *American Jewish World*, "Legacy of Pride," 86–89.

58. Here and below, see Gordon, *Jews in Transition*, 183; Nancy J. Schmidt, "An Orthodox Jewish Community in the United States: A Minority Within A Minority," in *Jewish Journal of Sociology*, 7:179–83 (December 1965); Plaut, *Jews in*

Minnesota, 174–76; Covner, "New Wilderness," 11; Chiat and Proshan, *We Rolled Up Our Sleeves*, 73–80.

59. Plaut, *Jews in Minnesota*, 292–94; Gordon, *Jews in Transition*, 24.

60. *Standard Club, 50th Anniversary Souvenir Book*, 21–24 ([Minneapolis, 1958]). Gordon cites 1921 as the date of the merger, but the anniversary book is more authoritative. On the name change, see Gordon, *Jews in Transition*, 62–64; *American Jewish World*, Aug. 10, 1945, p. 8, Sept. 7, 1945, p. 46, Oct. 19, 1945, p. 7.

61. Menorah Society of the University of Minnesota, *Annual*, 1926, 1–4, 1927, 11 ([Minneapolis], 1926, 1927), hereafter cited as *Menorah Annual*. Gordon, *Jews in Transition*, 25, and Plaut, *Jews in Minnesota*, 168, erroneously dated the origins of the Jewish Literary Society as 1905 and 1903, respectively.

62. *American Jewish World*, July 13, 1945, p. 1; *Menorah Annual*, 1927, 13–15, discussed the need for a Hillel House on campus; Gordon, *Jews in Transition*, 187; Chiat and Proshan, *We Rolled Up Our Sleeves*, 27–31, states that the first Hillel opened in 1943.

63. Rapp, in *Minnesota History*, 43:213–21.

64. United States, *Census*, 1930, *Population*, 2:360; Plaut, *Jews in Minnesota*, 298; Gordon, *Jews in Transition*, 175–78. Gordon claimed that the *Shabbosdige Post* began publishing in 1917 and lasted for three years, but Plaut's evidence for the 1921 beginning date is more conclusive.

65. Dubnow, *Jews in Russia*, 3:55–58. For a comprehensive study of the Bund, see Ezra Mendelsohn, *Class Struggle in the Pale: The Formative Years of the Jewish Workers Movement in Czarist Russia* (Cambridge, Mass., 1970).

66. Herz Burgin, "Kurtze Geshichte fun der Idisher Arbeter Bavegung in di Vereinigte Shtaten," in *Almanac: 10th Jubilee of the International Workers Order* (Yiddish), 222–66 (New York, 1940); Erickson and Lazarus, *Jewish Community*, ch. 12, p. 2; David P. Nord, "Minneapolis and the Pragmatic Socialism of Thomas Van Lear," in *Minnesota History*, 45:3 (Spring 1976).

67. Plaut, *Jews in Minnesota*, 224n; Gordon, *Jews in Transition*, 175–77. For a sample of meetings of Yiddish Socialists and the Workmen's Circle in Duluth, see *Labor Leader* (Duluth), Sept. 21, 1917, p. 10; *Truth* (Duluth), Nov. 16, 1917, p. 1, Feb. 22, 1918, p. 3, Mar. 8, 1918, p. 2. The *American Jewish World* throughout the 1920s, 1930s, and 1940s reported similar meetings in Minneapolis and St. Paul. For a general history, see Judah I. Shapiro, *The Friendly Society: A History of the Workmen's Circle* (New York, 1970).

The International Workers' Order (IWO), founded in 1930, was the left-wing counterpart to the Workmen's Circle. Branches in St. Paul, Minneapolis, and Duluth constituted the core of IWO organization in Minnesota, which lasted until destroyed by government action during the Cold War; see *Almanac: 10th Jubilee*, 576, 579; *New York Times*, June 26, 1951, p. 12.

68. The 30th anniversary of the Labor Lyceum was celebrated in December 1945, with Mayor Hubert H. Humphrey as the main speaker; *American Jewish World*, Dec. 7, 1945, p. 15; Burgin, in *Almanac: 10th Jubilee*, 245–48.

69. Here and two paragraphs below, see Plaut, *Jews in Minnesota*, 87–89, 248–53; Feingold, *Zion in America*, 244–49. For accounts of Minnesota Jews' efforts on behalf of coreligionists in the

war zones, see, for example, *American Jewish World*, May 26, 1916, pp. 657, 659, July 21, 1916, pp. 787, 794, June 13, 1919, p. 689, May 30, 1919, p. 656. On the activities of Minnesota Jews in the American Jewish Congress, see *American Jewish World*, Jan. 3, 1919, p. 303, Jan. 10, 1919, p. 307.

70. Feingold, *Zion in America*, 283. For local reactions to Nazi Germany's treatment of its Jews, see *American Jewish World*, Mar. 22, 1935, pp. 1, 4, and throughout the 1930s. See also Chapman, "To Do These Mitzvahs," 166.

71. Figures compiled from Displaced Persons Resettled in Minnesota, January 1949–April 1952, and Minnesota Displaced Persons Commission Files, both in Minnesota Public Welfare Department Records, State Archives, MHS; Minneapolis figures from *Newsletter of Jewish Family and Children's Service*, January 1952, in Minneapolis Section, National Council of Jewish Women Papers, MHS. Chapman, "To Do These Mitzvahs," 170–79, claims that DPs began arriving in 1946. For more on Jewish DPs, see Wischnitzer, *To Dwell in Safety*, 260–73.

72. Amy Sherman, "From Refugees to New Americans: How Holocaust Survivors Became Jewish Americans in the Twin Cities," college paper (no attribution), May 18, 1994, states that about 1,000 Jews were resettled (p. 17) and that the DPs were kept at arm's length by the settled Jewish community. For a fascinating discussion of the way the Holocaust has been used as a foreign-policy weapon in support of Israel after 1967, see Peter Novick, *The Holocaust in American Life* (Boston, 1999). For a refutation of Novick's arguments, see Yehuda Bauer, *Rethinking the Holocaust* (New Haven, 2001).

73. There is a vast literature on the Holocaust and its impact on American Jews; see, for example, Arthur D. Morse, *While Six Million Died: A Chronicle of American Apathy* (New York, 1968); Henry L. Feingold, *The Politics of Rescue: The Roosevelt Administration and the Holocaust, 1938-1945* (New Brunswick, N.J., 1970). *American Jewish World*, 1945–46, gave a dramatic account of Minnesota Jews' reactions.

74. Here and below, see Melvin I. Urofsky, *Louis D. Brandeis and the Progressive Tradition*, 87–103 (Boston, 1981); W. Gunther Plaut, "How Zionism Came to Minnesota," and Seymour Leventman, "Zionism in Minneapolis," both in Raphael Patai, ed., *Herzl Year Book*, 5:221–35, 237–46 (New York, 1963); Gordon, *Jews in Transition*, 26, 34, 37, 197, 306–8; Rhoda G. Lewin, "Some New Perspectives on the Jewish Immigrant Experience in Minneapolis: An Experiment in Oral History," 141–43, Ph.D. thesis, University of Minnesota, 1978. For more on Zionism, see Feingold, *Zion in America*, 194–207; Naomi W. Cohen, "The Reaction of Reform Judaism in America to Political Zionism (1897-1922)," in *Publications of the American Jewish Historical Society*, 40:361–94 (June 1951).

75. Schloff, *Prairie Dogs*, 201–5; Linda Mack Schloff, "Our Story: A History of Hadassah, St. Paul Chapter, 1913–1988" ([St. Paul], 1988). For Minneapolis Hadassah after 1945, see Schloff, "Building Community," 161–91. Regarding the founding of the Minneapolis Chapter, Gordon, *Jews in Transition*, 34–35, gives Deinard credit, but Mary Lebedoff wrote that the Self-Denial Club was the genesis of the group and that, by 1924, had affiliated with the national organization. See Lebedoff history, JHSUM. For a history of the national organization since its inception, see Mar-

lin Levin, *Balm in Gilead: The Story of Hadassah* (New York, 1973).

76. Plaut and Leventman, in *Herzl Year Book*, 5:221–35, 237–46; Gordon, *Jews in Transition*.

77. *American Jewish World*, Mar. 30, 1945, p. 18, Oct. 19, 1945, p. 1, Jan. 4, 1946, p. 4, June 21, 1946, p. 1, May 14, 1948, pp. 1, 3, 5, May 21, 1948, p. 7, June 9, 1967, pp. 1, 4, June 23, 1967, p. 1. On American Jewish support of Israel, see Gerald S. Strober, *American Jews: Community in Crisis* (Garden City, N.Y., 1974), 9–25.

78. Here and below, see Hyman Berman, "Political Antisemitism in Minnesota during the Great Depression," in *Jewish Social Studies*, 38:247–64 (Summer–Fall 1976).

Genis was the manager of the Twin Cities Amalgamated Clothing Workers Union, vice president of the national union, and, in the later 1930s, president of the Minnesota Industrial Union Congress. Finkelstein was the local leader of the Ladies' Garment Workers Union; on both men, see John R. Steelman, *Who's Who in Labor*, 111, 128 (New York, 1946). Latz was a leader of the Laundry Workers Union and the organizer of the United Labor Committee for Human Rights; see *Minneapolis Tribune*, Dec. 26, 1948, p. 12, *Minneapolis Labor Review*, Dec. 30, 1948, p. 1. All three were active in Farmer-Labor politics.

79. Here and below, see Charles I. Cooper, "The Minnesota Jewish Council in Historical Perspective, 1939–1953," 1–7, typescript, November 1953, copy in MHS; papers, reports, self-survey, conclusions, and recommendations of the Minneapolis Mayor's Council on Human Relations, in Papers of Hubert H. Humphrey, Douglas Hall, and the Jewish Community Relations Council—all MHS; *American Jewish World*, Apr. 6, p. 11, Apr. 13, p. 4, May 4, p. 4, Oct. 12, p. 4—all 1945, Aug. 9, p. 7, Aug. 30, pp. 4, 11, Feb. 8, p. 1—all 1946, Sept. 12, 1947, p. 7, Nov. 5, 1948, p. 1; Gordon, *Jews in Transition*, 55–58. For a short history of the JCRC, see Chiat and Proshan, *We Rolled Up Our Sleeves*, 39–47.

80. Carey McWilliams, "Minneapolis: The Curious Twin," in *Common Ground*, Autumn 1946, pp. 61–65; Norman Pollack, "Ignatius Donnelly on Human Rights: A Study of Two Novels," in *Mid-America*, 47:99–112 (April 1965); Gordon, *Jews in Transition*, 44–48, 64; Plaut, *Jews in Minnesota*, 273–77, 280; *American Jewish World*, Sept. 22, 1922, p. 54, Mar. 9, 1945, p. 1, Mar. 1, 1946, p. 5, Oct. 5, 1948, p. 7; Michael Rapp, "An Historical Overview of Anti-Semitism in Minnesota, 1920–1960," Ph.D. diss., University of Minnesota, 1977. Riley was minister of the First Baptist Church, and Rader was minister of the River Lake Tabernacle. For an evaluation of McWilliams's research and conclusions, see Plaut, *Jews in Minnesota*, 282–84.

81. Fred A. Lyon, *Mount Sinai Hospital of Minneapolis, Minnesota: A History* (Minneapolis, 1995). For more on the rationale for building the hospital and on the auxiliary, see Schloff, "Building Community," 94–124, especially 95–97.

82. Papers, reports, self-survey, conclusions, and recommendations of the Minneapolis Mayor's Council on Human Relations, Papers of Hubert H. Humphrey, Douglas Hall, and the Jewish Community Relations Council—all MHS; *American Jewish World*, Apr. 6, p. 11, Apr. 13, p. 4, May 4, p. 4, Oct. 12, p. 4—all 1945, Aug. 9, p. 7, Aug. 30, pp. 4, 11, Feb. 8, p. 1—all 1946, Sept. 12, 1947, p. 7, Nov. 5, 1948, p. 1; Gordon, *Jews in Transition*, 55–58.

83. Jewish Community Relations Council, Anti-Defamation League of Minnesota and the Dakotas, Annual Reports, 1975–80, in the agency's office, Minneapolis; Gordon, *Jews in Transition,* 54.

84. Plaut, *Jews in Minnesota,* 112, 259. For the national voting trends of Jews after 1930, see Stephan D. Isaacs, *Jews in American Politics,* 140–42, 150–56 (New York, 1974); for Minnesota patterns, see election-day editorials and news in *American Jewish World.*

85. Information on Cohen and Naftalin from St. Paul and Minneapolis mayor's offices, Feb. 19, 1981; *Minnesota Legislative Manual 1979–1980,* 438 (St. Paul, [1979]), *1999–2000,* 316 (St. Paul, [1999]).

86. Plaut, *Mount Zion,* 93; Kramer and Leventman, *Children of the Gilded Ghetto,* 46, 48. To be sure they did crop up; for example, the Minneapolis Jewish Federation's decided not to continue funding institutions held sacred by Orthodoxy, such as the Jewish Sheltering Home (later called the Oak Park Home for Children) and the Hachnosses Orchim, a home for transient Jews. For an illuminating discussion, see Chapman, "To Do These Mitzvahs," 186–231.

87. Here and below, see Gordon, *Jews in Transition,* 6, 9, 292, 294; Erickson and Lazarus, *Jewish Community,* ch. 5, p. 8. The Jewish poor have been a singularly invisible part of the community, except during times like the Great Depression, when charitable organizations were overwhelmed; Rutman, "Defense and Development," 98–102.

88. Erickson and Lazarus, *Jewish Community,* ch. 4, pp. 3–7; *American Jewish World,* Sept. 9, 1966, p. 28, Dec. 30, 1966, p. 3.

89. Schloff, "Building Community," 94–191, and *Prairie Dogs,* 191–224. See also collections of Minneapolis and St. Paul sections of National Council of Jewish Women, of Mount Sinai Hospital Women's Auxiliary, and of Minneapolis, St. Paul, and regional Hadassah—JHSUM.

90. Here and below, see Kramer and Leventman, *Children of the Gilded Ghetto,* 129–50; Erickson and Lazarus, *Jewish Community,* ch. 5, pp. 9–11, 18, 20, 30, 32.

91. Covner, "New Wilderness," 22; Proshan, "Eastern European Jewish Immigrants and Their Children," 290–336.

92. Here and below, see Erickson and Lazarus, *Jewish Community,* ch. 7, pp. 3, 4, ch. 13, pp. 2, 6, 13–15.

93. U.S., *Census,* 1970, *Population,* vol. 1, part 25, p. 514; Gordon, *Jews in Transition,* 106, 168.

94. St. Paul and Minneapolis community surveys, JHSUM.

95. Statistics on numbers of Jews from the former Soviet Union are unreliable. Those sent to Schloff by Hebrew Immigrant Aid Society do not agree with those of the Jewish Family Services although they are supposedly dealing with the same group of people. Adding to this conundrum is the fact that people who did not receive refugee status were never officially counted. Statistics collected by Russian-owned businesses and a cultural association indicate that as many as 50,000 Russian-speaking people live here. These include Pentecostals and others who are not Jewish but who often use Jewish services because they know they will find Russian speakers available.

96. Coupled with anti-Semitism as a motive for emigrating was the constricting choice of educational opportunities for children in Russia. Schloff is indebted

to Asya Fridland, supervisor of resettlement services at Jewish Family and Children's Service of Minneapolis, for her conversation on June 15, 2001, and to Marina Star and Gail Saeks, resettlement case manager and program manager for the Vocational and Resettlement Department at Jewish Family Service of St. Paul on May 16, 2001. The information is also based on 20 oral history interviews conducted by Linda Mack Schloff under a 1991 research grant from the Minnesota Historical Society. The project included many conversations with Felicia Weingarten, who was the contact in the community. Tapes are in possession of Schloff.

See also Paul Ellenbogen and Stephen C. Feinstein, "Soviet Emigres in Saint Paul: Some Reflections on the Absorption Process" (St. Paul, 1981); they found that while in Russia 33% celebrated Chanukah, 56% observed Passover, and 33% attended synagogues. Stephen C. Feinstein, "Aspects of Integrating Soviety Jewish Immigrants in America: Attitudes of American Jewry Toward the Recent Immigration," in a report to the St. Paul United Jewish Fund and Council, 1981, found that the existing St. Paul Jewish community was not particularly hospitable to the newcomers. Both papers in possession of Schloff. Personal observance of Schloff for synagogue attendance in Twin Cities and perusal of synagogue newsletters for Russian Jews' bar and bat mitzvahs.

For a discussion of client/institution problems, see also Steven J. Gold, "Dealing with Frustration: A Study of Interactions Between Resettlement Staff and Refugees," in Scott M. Morgan and Elizabeth Colson, eds., *People in Upheaval* (Staten Island, 1987). For commemoration of Jewish life-cycle events, see Fran

Markowitz, "Ritual as Keys to Soviet Immigrants' Jewish Identity," 128–47, in Jack Kugelmass, ed., *Between Two Worlds: Ethnographic Essays on American Jewry* (Ithaca, 1988).

97. Gary Tobin, *Jewish Population Study of Greater Saint Paul 1993*, 17 (St. Paul, 1993); Project Research, Inc., *Community Profile: Prepared for the Minneapolis Federation for Jewish Service*, 5 (Minneapolis, 1994); Erickson and Lazarus, *Jewish Community*, ch. 1, p. 1.

98. Tobin, *St. Paul*, 17–18; Project Research, Inc., *Minneapolis*, 20–24.

99. Tobin, *St. Paul*, 30–39; Project Research, Inc., *Minneapolis*, 30–34.

100. For synagogue and voluntarism, see Tobin, *St. Paul*, 70–72, 85–88; Project Research, Inc., *Minneapolis*, 57–61, 91–96.

101. For quote, see [Minneapolis] Jewish Community Profile summary, August 1994, p. 1. For type of religion and intermarriage, see Tobin, *St. Paul*, 50, 54–56; Project Research, Inc., *Minneapolis*, 15, 36–37, 42–49.

102. Tobin, *St. Paul*, 49–53, 57–60; Project Research, Inc., *Minneapolis*, 55.

103. Pessimists include Arthur Hertzberg, *The Jews in America: Four Centuries of an Uneasy Encounter: A History* (New York, 1989); he posits that Jews can no longer define themselves by fear and exclusion. They have to find new sources of meaning and value by linking themselves to the intellectual and spiritual traditions so long neglected. See also Charles Liebman, *The Ambivalent American Jew* (Philadelphia, 1978). Just slightly less pessimistic are Samuel C. Heilman, *Portrait of American Jews: The Last Half of the 20th Century* (Seattle, 1995), and Mary Waters, *Ethnic Options: Choosing Ethnic Identities in America* (Berkeley, 1990).

104. It is too soon to say if these programs are making a difference. One program, however, called "A Taste of Judaism," aimed at intermarried couples, has had attendance as high as 160 per session people in 2001. Rabbi Hayim Herring, "Taking Strides Toward Jewish Continuity: An Executive Summary of Continuity Activities," Minneapolis Jewish Federation paper, Mar. 23, 1998; "Identity & Continuity, 2001–2002 Budget Narrative, May 7, 2001"; "Dare to Dream: A Road Map for Innovation in Community Education," Feb. 4, 1997; "Kehilla Committee Executive Summary: Strategic Planning for Jewish Education," Aug. 27, 1998—all produced by the Minneapolis Jewish Federation. Rabbi Hayim Herring and Nancy Leffert, "Analysis: A New Jewish Identity in Formation?" in *Agenda: Jewish Education*, 9: 8–12 (Fall 1997)—all JHSUM. Schloff is indebted to Rabbi Herring, assistant executive director of Minneapolis Jewish Federation, for sharing them and for the conversation of June 14, 2001.

105. For an ethnographic analysis of two Twin Cities Conservative synagogues, see Riv Ellen Prell, "Communities of Choice and Memory: Conservative Synagogues in the Late Twentieth Century," 269–358, in *Jews in the Center: Conservative Synagogues and their Members*, Jack Wertheimer, ed. (Rutgers, 2000). Internet learning is common through synagogue e-mail and Jewish web sites.

106. This sect, tracing its origins to an 18th-century eastern European pietistic revival, attempts to persuade all Jews to perform all ritual functions and family obligations in a context of joy. The Minnesota group is part of a worldwide movement, looking to the Lubavitcher Rebbe for guidance. A Lubavitch day school was established in St. Paul in 1976, Bais Yakov, a high school for girls, opened in 1996–97, and a Yeshiva or institutue of higher learning in the 1990s. Their Bais Chanah, established in 1971, draws women seeking spiritual fulfillment from all over the world. For Bais Chanah, see Lynn Davidman, *Tradition in a Rootless World: Women Turn to Orthodox Judaism* (Berkeley, 1991); Edward Hoffman, *Despite All Odds: The Story of Lubavitch* (New York, 1991). See also Feingold, *Zion in America*, 309; Strober, *American Jews*, 260–64. Alexander Dillon, "Outreach and Community: The Lubavitcher Hassidim of St. Paul," undergraduate paper, Macalester College, Spring 1990, copy in JHSUM. Phone conversation with Rabbi Moshe Feller on July 19, 2001; Schloff is indebted to him for providing an undated article, "An Overview of Upper Midwest Merkos-Chabad Lubavitch."

107. Jewish Community Action newsletter, *T'kiah*, Winter, Summer 2000, Winter, Spring 2001; JCRC, "Celebrating 60 Years of Protecting Jewish Interests and Promoting Jewish Ideals, 1998." Steven Silverfarb, the executive director, in a telephone conversation on July 18, 2001, related that there were about 30 cases of anti-Semitism brought to the attention of the JCRC in 2000. Despite the low number, one troubling case involved findings of persistent anti-Semitism among faculty members at St. Cloud State University. See also Jewish Community Relations Council of Minnesota and the Dakotas Annual Report, 1998.

Index

Page numbers in italic refer to pictures and captions.

Picture Credits

Names of the photographers, when known, are in parentheses following the page number on which the picture appears.

Minnesota Historical Society—page x, 3, 6 (*Northwest Magazine*, February 1888, p. 30), 14 (both; bottom, Joseph Zalusky), 15, 19 (bottom), 21 (both), 23, 25, 27, 29 (bottom), 30, 34 (bottom), 37, (bottom), 50, 53 (*Minneapolis Star-Journal*), 55 (Mark Jensen), 71, 74

Jewish Historical Society of the Upper Midwest—page 16, 17 (both), 19 (top), 20, 22, 24, 28, 29 (top), 31, 34 (top), 35, 36 (both), 37 (top), 39, 41, 45, 46 (Ostrin-Steinberg Studios, Minneapolis), 48, 51, 54, 56, 66

Herzl Camp, Webster, Wisc.—page 47

Bette Globus Goodman—page 61

Hillel, Minneapolis—page 64 (Amy Olson)

Jewish Community Action, St. Paul—page 67

Acknowledgments

I wish to thank the following people for aiding me in bringing this story up to the present. Rabbi Hayim Herring, assistant executive director of the Minneapolis Jewish Federation; Marina Star, resettlement case manager, and Gail Saeks, program manager, Vocational and Resettlement Department at Jewish Family Service of St. Paul; and Asya Fridland, supervisor of resettlement services at the Jewish Family and Children's Service of Minneapolis, met with me at various times to discuss their areas of expertise. Rabbi David Freedman of Rochester and Joanne Sher of Duluth were most helpful as well. I also held a fruitful telephone conversation with Steven Silverfarb, director of the Jewish Community Relations Council. Herzl Camp, Hillel, and Jewish Community Action promptly made photos available to us. Marilyn Chiat deserves credit for her heroic work in documenting Jewish life in Minnesota's smaller towns.

I thank all the people who have donated materials to the Jewish Historical Society of the Upper Midwest. In doing so they have made it a major repository for regional Jewish history. Finally I want to thank MHS intern Ben Petry for his photo research and editor Sally Rubinstein for her sensitive editing and willingness to locate materials I could not supply.

Linda Mack Schloff

Minnesotans can trace their families and their state's heritage to a multitude of ethnic groups. *The People of Minnesota* series tells each group's story in a compact, handsomely illustrated, and accessible paperback. Readers will learn about the group's accomplishments, ethnic organizations, settlement patterns, and occupations. Each book includes a personal story of one person or family, told through a diary, a letter, or an oral history.

In his introduction to the series, Bill Holm reminds us why these stories are as important as ever: "To be ethnic, somehow, is to be human. Neither can we escape it, nor should we want to. You cannot interest yourself in the lives of your neighbors if you don't take sufficient interest in your own."

This series is based on the critically acclaimed book *They Chose Minnesota: A Survey of the State's Ethnic Groups* (Minnesota Historical Society Press). The volumes in *The People of Minnesota* bring each group's story up to date and add dozens of photographs to inform and enhance the telling.

Books in the series include *Irish in Minnesota, Jews in Minnesota, Norwegians in Minnesota,* and *African Americans in Minnesota.*

Bill Holm is the grandson of four Icelandic immigrants to Minneota, Minnesota, where he still lives. He is the author of eight books including *Eccentric Island: Travels Real and Imaginary* and *Coming Home Crazy.* When he is not practicing the piano or on the road circuit-riding for literature, he teaches at Southwest State University in Marshall, Minnesota.

About the Authors

Hyman Berman is professor emeritus at the University of Minnesota and co-author of *The American Worker in the Twentieth Century: A History through Autobiographies.*

Linda Mack Schloff is director of the Jewish Historical Society of the Upper Midwest and author of *"And Prairie Dogs Weren't Kosher": Jewish Women in the Upper Midwest Since 1855.*

Printed in the USA
CPSIA information can be obtained
at www.ICGtesting.com
JSHW082222140824
68134JS00015B/690